British Orders, Decorations
and Medals

British Orders, Decorations and Medals

by

Donald Hall

in association with

Christopher Wingate

A Balfour Book, printed and published by Photo Precision Ltd.,
St. Ives, Huntingdon, England

ACKNOWLEDGEMENTS

The authors are most grateful to the following for the loan of medals, for permission to quote certain figures on the awards of Gallantry Decorations and Medals, for permission to reproduce from paintings, and for general assistance in the preparation of this book.

British Gallantry Awards by Abbott and Tamplin published by Guinness Superlatives Limited
Gallantry Awards by C. J. K. Wingate published by Spink & Son Limited in their Numismatic Circular
Imperial War Museum
National Army Museum
National Maritime Museum, Greenwich
P. E. Abbott Esq.,
P. Gaston Esq.,
Professor R. H. Graveson, C.B.E.
E. C. Joslin Esq.,
J. M. A. Tamplin Esq.,
Miss Carol Hall (for typing and checking the MS.)

FIRST EDITION 1973

SECOND EDITION 1974

©

ISBN 0 85944 000 1

Foreword

by Sir John Smyth V.C.

I am constantly astonished that in this last quarter of the 20th Century there should be so much interest in past campaigns and the medals that go with them.

To my mind the great merit of this Balfour book, which is excellently printed and produced, is that it sets out the British Orders, Decorations and Medals in simple form. The all-coloured campaign medals are unique – and without colour any medal can look rather drab and difficult to recognise. The battle illustrations are vivid and attractive. The book covers 200 years of British history and is highly educative and interesting from that point of view alone. All these things will make it attractive to young people and others who do not pretend to be collectors or experts on the subject. The book should be most suitable for School libraries.

I am on record as being strongly opposed to the present traffic in V.C.s, many of which, having been purchased perhaps from penurious relatives for a trifling sum, are sold and resold at public auctions for private gain. This will continue until it becomes recognised that the deed which won the medal is of much more importance than the medal itself.

There have recently been hundreds of imitation V.C.s manufactured in Britain and sold to people both here and in the United States; but they very soon lose their attraction as they are not connected with a particular V.C. We have also had quite a number of bogus V.C.s (no names no pack drill!), but these are disappearing as the living holders become fewer – and more conspicuous.

At the 1956 Centenary V.C. Re-union a badly disabled V.C. in the Star and Garter Home, who had sold his V.C. for a trifling sum (a very unusual occurrence for a living holder of the medal), wrote to me and asked if he could have a duplicate to allow him to attend the parade. I got the War Office to give a mock-up V.C. just for the occasion and he wore it as he was pushed past the Queen in his wheel chair. I see nothing wrong in that. But another man was also pushed past wearing an imitation V.C., who was not a V.C. at all – and I see everything wrong in that.

It used to be said – quite wrongly – that 'Old soldiers never die, they simply fade away'. This is more true of old medals, all of which have meant, or still mean, something to someone – whether it be the winner of the medal or his relatives and descendants. Old campaign medals of course become dated and are replaced by others, but the deliberate closing down of a medal, whilst a number of its holders are still alive, must always be a sad occasion for some. Medals are for people, and it is the people who win the medal - and their deeds of gallantry - which are of more importance than the medal itself. The medal merely commemorates what they have done. And it should never be thought that, because one Victoria Cross fetches more money in an auction than another that the deed of gallantry of the lesser in cash value was in any way inferior. The Crosses themselves are made from an old Russian cannon captured in the Crimean War and one V.C. is just the same as another, with the exception of course of the inscription on the back. They are made solely by that highly reputable firm of Messrs Hancock and Co.

I had my own V.C. stolen many years ago, but I wear the duplicate with which I was provided with equal pride. When King George V decorated me with my V.C. in July 1915 he gave me a very cheap little cardboard box (which I still treasure) to go with it, saying: "I give you this highest decoration of all in this very ordinary box so that the intrinsic value of the medal and the box shall not be more than one penny".

At the only medal auction I have ever attended, a few years ago, an Indian Mutiny Naval V.C. was purchased by ex-Naval Officer John Bartholomew for £3,500 – and he immediately presented it to the Maritime Museum. The fantastic price is at least an indication of the ever-increasing interest the public and the collectors take in medals.

Amongst the medals listed in this book, the following bring back personal memories for me: the Mons Star won by 'The Old Contemptibles' who took the first shock of the German Army at the beginning of the First World War; and the Burma Star, immortalised by Field Marshall Bill Slim and his 14th Army, in the Second. What tremendous comradeship there was – and still is – amongst the holders of these two Stars. The Old Contemptibles have had their last parade, but the Burma Star still shines with increasing brightness – despite the sad death of my friend, Bill Slim, himself.

Then there is the Indian General Service Medal 1908–1935 with its twelve bars, of which *my* five include the Frontier Campaign against the Mahsuds in 1919–20, the toughest frontier campaign in which the British have ever been engaged; and the final bar 'North-west Frontier 1935,' the campaign against the Mohmands, in which Auchinleck commanded the Force, Alexander commanded a brigade and I commanded a battalion. This was the campaign in which Field Marshal Auchinleck (then a temporary Major-General) first made his reputation as a commander, and tanks were first used on the North-west Frontier.

Then the Distinguished Conduct Medal, founded by Queen Victoria in 1845 (eleven years before the Victoria Cross). I succeeded Field Marshal Lord Wilson as President of the D.C.M. League in 1958 and held that office for twelve years. Grand old soldiers these D.C.M.s – many of them very near misses for the Victoria Cross. They should certainly have been awarded the £100 annual gratuity.

The Royal Red Cross, founded in 1883 by Queen Victoria, was awarded to those wonderful Queen Alexandra's Nurses, who gave such outstanding service in the care of the sick or wounded in the fighting services. I got to know the famous Q.A.s when I wrote THE WILL TO LIVE, the life story of their one-time Matron-in-Chief, Dame Margot Turner.

And finally, our two highest decorations for gallantry, the Victoria Cross and the George Cross. The Victoria Cross was founded by Queen Victoria in 1856 for supreme gallantry in the face of the enemy and ante-dated two years to include the Crimean War. It has remained as our highest British decoration and is generally regarded as supreme amongst the medals of the world. As this book says, the ribbon was originally blue for the Royal Navy and crimson for the Army. A few years ago I was invited to attend the unveiling of a picture in the Buckingham Palace Gallery depicting the first-ever V.C. investiture on 26th June, 1857 in Hyde Park where sixty-two Crosses were presented by Her Majesty Queen Victoria. In the picture the Queen was shown presenting a red-ribboned V.C. to a sailor. Everyone asked me how this awful error had happened. I replied that I was quite sure that neither Queen Victoria nor the Secretary of State for War, who handed her the medal, could have perpetrated such an atrocity and that the artist, who perhaps wasn't in the know, just painted the blue ribbon red.

I have attended every V.C. Re-union – the first one in 1920, immediately after the First World War; in 1929, when the Prince of Wales gave his historic dinner in the House of Lords; and the present Queen's Centenary Re-union of the V.C.s in 1956. It was during that Re-union that the V.C.s asked me to form a V.C. Association which the holders of the George Cross were invited to join a few years later. And every other year since then the V.C. and G.C. Association has held a Re-union in London with the assistance of the Government of the day and the Royal Air Force.

At the time of writing (February 1973) there are only 146 V.C.s alive, 72 of whom are First World War and in their middle seventies. No-one would wish for more V.C.s to be awarded, as it is essentially a battle decoration, and we don't want any more wars, but at the Imperial War Museum in London and in Canada, Australia and New Zealand, V.C. memorial centres have been established.

No British medal has had such an eventful short history as the George Cross. Its institution was announced on 23rd September, 1940 by King George VI as a new and very high decoration to be awarded to men and women for acts of supreme gallantry – not on the field of battle – and to be worn immediately after the V.C. It was also announced that the new medal would be given an immediate 'blood transfusion' from the ranks of the Empire Gallantry Medal, all the 112 living holders of which were authorised to exchange their E.G.M.s for G.C.s. Curiously enough, the G.C.s awarded during the six years of war also numbered 112, some two-thirds of them being post-humous. In the 26 years since the war, only 31 G.C.s have been awarded, making a total of 143.

On 22nd October 1971 Prime Minister Edward Heath announced in the House of Commons another massive blood transfusion to the G.C., when the living holders of the Albert and Edward Medals, some 122 in all, were authorised to exchange their medals for George Crosses. These gallant holders of the Empire Gallantry, Albert and Edward Medals, who are now G.C.s, have been warmly welcomed into my V.C. and G.C. Association, and we celebrated together a historic Re-union in London in 1972, which was attended both by Princess Anne and Her Majesty Queen Elizabeth the Queen Mother. I am indeed very proud and honoured to have been both Chairman and President of such a wonderful Association. What the G.C. requires now is one or two new awards each year and with the spread of violence in civil life increasing throughout Britain and various parts of the British Commonwealth there would be ample grounds for these.

I have found in my life that the bravest people are usually the most humble – and I class humility as one of the greatest virtues. I think that all my colleagues in the V.C. and G.C. Association realise that there are many others who have deserved our awards as much or more than we have – but perhaps because no one was watching, or for some other reason, their gallant deed went unhonoured and unsung.

Jackie Smyth

Introduction

It is with considerable pleasure that I write this short introduction to the second edition of our book and, in doing so, would like to thank all those who have been kind enough to send comments and corrections. In the latter respect we are particularly indebted to Lt. Col. M. A. Demetriadi, Mr. J. Granger, Mr. Alec Purves, Mr. John Tamplin and Mr. Geoffrey Whitehead. If any names have inadvertently been omitted we offer our apologies to those concerned and hasten to add that we are equally grateful to them.

The main purpose of our book was to make an already popular hobby even more so by bringing it to the notice of the layman as, quite obviously, a work of this kind can only be of limited interest to the established collector. It is, therefore, a source of great satisfaction to know that the primary objective has been achieved. Over seven thousand copies have already been sold, thus making it possible to produce this second edition. The rapidly increasing interest from collectors overseas, mainly, of course, from English speaking countries, is confirmed by the significant number of copies sold to them. This can only prove beneficial to collectors everywhere because, whilst the true collector is not really concerned about financial gain, he is forced to consider this aspect on account of continually increasing prices which world wide demand can only stimulate.

For the benefit of new readers I quote several extracts from the introduction to the first edition which outline some aspects of medal collecting.

To the newcomer there may be many anomalies in the hobby that are not easily explained.

Why, for instance, does a Waterloo medal cost around £50, whilst the Mons Star costs only as many shillings? Both had a tremendous influence on the future of Great Britain. I think that one must bear in mind the fact that the two actions are almost one hundred years apart in time. In that period, inevitably, many Waterloo medals have just disappeared from the market, many permanently in that they have become lost or destroyed and others only temporarily in that over the years they have gone into the cabinets of collectors; in the latter case we may presume that they may eventually once again come into the market.

Another question which may well be raised is that of condition. Any coin or stamp collector will know, in those particular hobbies, that condition is of prime importance. A scratch or knock on an otherwise flawless coin or a thinned back or a damaged perforation on a stamp can drastically reduce the value or even make it absolutely valueless.

This does not apply with anything like such severity in medal collecting. Medals were intended to be worn, and in days gone by were worn proudly by the recipients much more frequently than is the case today. Consequently they became rubbed, knocked and generally worn. Because of its attractive appearance a mint condition medal *will* command a premium over and above its normal value, but such a premium will be small, maybe between five and ten per cent . . . that is unless the medal is in mint condition because the recipient was killed in action and thus had little or no chance to wear it! In such a case the value will jump many times.

For instance, a Zulu medal with clasp '1877–8–9' to an ordinary regiment of foot will cost you around £23. If you should have the good fortune to discover that the recipient of that medal was killed at the famous action at Rorke's Drift then that value will jump to above £200, which proves that research pays handsome dividends.

Certain medals, whilst common to some regiments, are rare to others. In the first case perhaps the whole regiment took part in the campaign and thus many hundreds were entitled to the medal: in the second the medal, although exactly similar, may have been awarded to some specialist on attachment such as signaller, chaplain or farrier.

Thus the value is increased because of the rarity, *not of the medal*, but of the medal to the particular regiment from which the specialist was on loan.

What do you collect? This is largely a matter of individual taste. Many people try to make a collection of 'one of each', i.e. one example of each type of campaign medal issued; others take one particular medal and try to obtain one example to each regiment entitled to that particular medal, whilst others specialise in a particular regiment, or medals to the R.A.F. or Royal Navy.

But whatever you do, may I ask one favour of you? Please, *never* split up a group of medals to one man. You will find that most dealers strongly deprecate this practice, and there are many collectors who literally spend a lifetime trying to complete a group which has been split up years before by some thoughtless individual who detached and sold, perhaps, the Long Service and Good Conduct Medal because, 'I don't collect LSGC medals!'

How to obtain medals to start one's collection could be the subject of a book on its own, but suffice it to say that the new collector would be well advised to confine his purchases from those who give some form of guarantee with their merchandise. In the early days of his collecting he is likely to make mistakes in some of the pieces that he purchases but at least if he buys as I have suggested he will, in the event of any piece not being what it purports to be, be assured of a refund of his purchase money.

True, the professional dealer is far less likely to let a rarity slip through his stock at normal price but it *does* happen from time to time. Dealers are busy people and it would be impossible for them to check and verify every single item which passes through their hands, and it is here that the specialist can eventually make his study pay off.

With the greatly increased interest in British orders, decorations and medals, there are now more dealers and, as it could prove helpful to the new collector, a number of them are listed below in alphabetical order. The fact that a firm is not mentioned does not imply that it is less reliable than those that are and no indication of preference or other differentiation is intended.

A. H. Baldwin & Sons Ltd.,
11 Adelphi Terrace,
London WC2N 6BJ

A. D. Hamilton & Co.,
7 St. Vincent Place,
Glasgow, G1 2DW

Kenneth C. Lovell,
22a Church Lane,
Leytonstone,
London E11

Spink & Son Ltd.,
5–7 King Street,
St. James's,
London SW1

Clark & Scott,
55 Princes Road,
Middlesbrough,
Teesside, TS1 4BG

J. B. Hayward & Son,
17 Piccadilly Arcade,
London, SW1Y 5NL

Charles A. Lusted,
96a Calverley Road,
Tunbridge Wells,
Kent, TN1 2UN

Donald Hall,
108 Blindmans Lane,
Cheshunt, Herts,
EN8 9DN

Lanham's Exchanges,
26 Earl Street,
Coventry, Warwicks.

B. A. Seaby Ltd.,
Audley House,
11 Margaret Street,
London, W1N 8AT

I hope that this book will continue to stimulate interest in this most fascinating of hobbies and, to further this objective, the authors will continue to welcome comments, criticisms and suggestions because, although every effort has been made to rectify errors contained in the first edition, they are only too well aware that mistakes could still come to light.

Donald Hall

PART ONE

Orders of Chivalry

Opposite: The Order of the Garter procession. Founded in 1348,
this is Britain's most ancient order of chivalry.

The Most Noble Order of the Garter

This is the premier Order of Chivalry and was founded by Edward III. The exact date of foundation is uncertain but is generally accepted to have been 1348.

The Order is one class only and consists of the Sovereign and twenty-five Knights-Companions. In addition foreign Royalty may be admitted as extra Knights.

The insignia comprises the Garter, the Collar, the Star, the George and the Lesser George. The Garter is worn below the left knee, or in the case of Royal ladies of the Order, on the left arm between the shoulder and elbow. The Collar, which is of gold and is of 30 ozs. troy-weight, consists of twenty-four linked red roses within a representation of the Garter, the Star is eight pointed and of chipped silver, the George is gold and is a representation of St. George slaying the dragon and is suspended from the Collar, and the "Lesser George" which is worn suspended by the sash ribbon on the right hip. In addition, there is the mantle, the hood, the surcoat and the hat.

This very high honour has in recent times, with that of the Thistle, been within the personal gift of the Sovereign and not on the recommendation of the Prime Minister. Since the war there have been processions in connection with the installation of Knights of the Garter at St. George's Chapel, Windsor.

The Most Ancient and the Most Noble Order of the Thistle

The original foundation is unknown, though believed to have been in the fifteenth century. James II revived the Order by a Warrant dated 29th May, 1687. In 1703 Queen Anne re-established the Order in its present form and it now consists of the Sovereign and sixteen Knights, though this number may be increased by members of the Royal family. The insignia consists of the Star, which is a combination of a St. Andrew's cross and a four-pointed star, the Collar which is of gold and enamel, and the Badge which is worn from the Collar and is a gold representation of St. Andrew carrying a white enamelled St. Andrew's cross. In addition, there is a mantle of dark green velvet and a hat of black velvet.

In normal full dress the Badge is worn on a riband passing over the left shoulder to the right hip with the Star attached to the coat. The Chapel of the Order is in the High Kirk of St. Giles, Edinburgh.

The Most Illustrious Order of St. Patrick

Established by King George III in 1783 as a National Order for Ireland, this Order has not been awarded since the political changes in 1922. The Order of St. Patrick is again a one class Order consisting of the Sovereign and twenty-two Knights-Companions.

As in the case of the Order of the Thistle, the insignia consists of the Collar, the Star and the Badge. In addition, there is a mantle, hat and surcoat.

The collar is of gold composed of roses and harps placed alternate and linked with knots of gold; in the centre there is an Imperial Crown surmounting a harp of gold. The Badge is oval and of gold and is surrounded with a wreath of shamrock within which is a circle of sky-blue enamel containing the motto *Quis separabit*.

The Star of the Order consists of the cross of St. Patrick on a field argent, surmounted by a trefoil vert charged with three imperial crowns and surrounded by the same motto.

In full dress when the Mantle and Collar are not worn, the Star and Badge are worn as for the Order of the Thistle, except that the riband is worn over the right shoulder, the Badge on the left hip.

The Most Honourable Order of the Bath

Originally established as a military Order, it is believed in 1399. The unusual name of this Order probably emanates from the practice of including ablutions as one of the symbolic rituals of initiation to knighthood. The Order was revived in 1725 and was considerably enlarged at the close of the Napoleonic wars and was reconstituted in three classes. A civil division was founded by Queen Victoria in 1847 and the Order was opened to women in 1971.

The Order now consists of three classes in both divisions. The classes are Knights or Dames Grand Cross (G.C.B.), Knights or Dames Commanders (K. or D.C.B.), and Companions (C.B.).

On ceremonial occasions the Knights or Dames Grand Cross wear the Badge, either civil or military, from the Collar of gold which consists of crowns, roses, thistles and shamrocks, linked together by knots, and the Star is worn on the left. The mantles, when worn, are of crimson satin lined with white taffeta and on the left side is an embroidered representation of the Star.

Knights Commanders wear the Badge suspended from a riband round the neck and the Badge is somewhat smaller than those of Knights Grand Cross. Dames Commanders wear a similar Badge suspended from a bow from the left shoulder. In addition both Knights and Dames Commanders wear a slightly smaller Star on the left breast. Companions of either sex have no Star and the Badge is worn in the case of a man suspended from a riband round the neck and in the case of a lady from a bow on the left shoulder.

Unlike the first three Orders of Chivalry, the riband of this Order and all subsequent Orders may be worn in undress uniform.

The Most Exalted Order of the Star of India

This Order was instituted by Queen Victoria on the 23rd February, 1861 and was given precedence above that of the Order of St. Michael and St. George. The Order is now obsolescent and no appointments have been made since the Independence of India in 1947. The appointments to the Order were made from ruling princes and chiefs of India and British subjects who had done service of note in India.

The Order is a three-class Order consisting of Knights Grand Commanders (G.C.S.I.), Knights Commanders (K.C.S.I.), and Companions (C.S.I.). (The expression "Knights Grand Commanders" instead of "Knights Grand Cross" was chosen for this Order and that of the Indian Empire to avoid embarrassment to recipients of non-Christian faith).

The Grand Master of the Order was always the Viceroy of India.

The insignia of this Order in the first class are more beautiful and valuable than those of any other Order as they are ornamented with a considerable number of diamonds, and are worn in full dress uniform with the Star on the left breast, the Badge on the left hip. Knights Commanders and Companions wear insignia in the same style as for the Order of the Bath.

The Most Distinguished Order of St. Michael and St. George

This Order was founded on the 27th April, 1818 by the Prince Regent on behalf of his father, King George III. Like the Order of the Bath it consists of three classes; also like the Order of the Bath it is open to both men and women. The three classes consist of Knights or Dames Grand Cross (G.C.M.G.), Knight or Dame Commanders (K. or D.C.M.G.), and Companions (C.M.G.). This Order has, since the institution of the Order of the British Empire in 1917, been reserved very largely for diplomats, members of the Foreign Service and for those who have performed valuable administrative services in connection with the Commonwealth.

Knights or Dames Grand Cross on all great occasions wear mantles of saxon-blue satin lined with scarlet silk. On the left side of the mantle is a representation of the Star of the Order.

The Collar of the Order is composed of lions of England, of Maltese crosses and of the cyphers "S.M." and "S.G.". In the centre of the Collar there is an imperial crown of two winged lions, each holding in his fore-paw a book and seven arrows.

The Badge of the Order, which is an enamelled white cross of fourteen points, has on one side the same design as that of the Star and on the other side a representation of St. George armed with a sword and encountering a dragon.

When Knights or Dames Grand Cross do not wear the Collar, the Badge is suspended from a four inches wide saxon-blue riband with a scarlet central stripe, passing from the right shoulder to the left hip.

Knights or Dames Commanders receive no collars but similar, though smaller, badges and stars. The Companions receive badges only. Both Knights Commanders and Companions wear their badges around the neck, Dames Commanders or Lady Companions on a bow from the left shoulder.

23

The Most Eminent Order of the Indian Empire

This Order was originally founded on the 1st January, 1878 as a one class Order which had a badge only, similar to that of the subsequent badge but with the word India spelt out on the petals.

Queen Victoria founded the Order to commemorate her assumption of the title Empress of India.

On the 2nd August, 1886 the Order was reconstituted as a junior Order to that of the Star of India and was in three classes consisting of Knights Grand Commanders (G.C.I.E.), Knights Commanders (K.C.I.E.) and Companions (C.I.E.).

The first class was reserved for those persons who by their services to the Empire of India merited royal favour and for distinguished Eastern potentates.

No appointments to the Order have been made since 1947.

The Viceroy of India was always the Grand Master of the Order.

The Royal Victorian Order

This Order was founded by Queen Victoria in 1896 and unlike those Orders to which appointments are made on the recommendation of the Prime Minister, are entirely in the personal gift of the Sovereign. Awards in the various classes are made for personal services to the Sovereign. The Order consists of five classes and is open to both men and women.

The five classes are as follows:–

    Knights or Dames Grand Cross (G.C.V.O.).
    Knights or Dames Commanders (K. or D.C.V.O.).
    Commanders (C.V.O.).
    Members, Fourth Class (M.V.O.).
    Members Fifth Class (M.V.O.).

In addition there is a medal to the Order in silver-gilt, silver and bronze.

The mantles of Knights and Dames Grand Cross are of dark blue silk edged with red satin and lined with white silk and fastened by a cordon of dark blue silk and gold. On the left side of the mantle is a representation of the Star of the Order. The Collar of the Order is of gold and the Badge consists of a white enamelled Maltese cross of eight points, in the centre of which is the Royal imperial monogram of Queen Victoria, in gold, and the motto of the Order, *Victoria*, with the imperial crown enamelled in proper colours.

Knights and Dames Grand Cross, Knights and Dames Commanders, Companions and lady Companions wear insignia as for the Order of St. Michael and St. George. The badges of the fourth and fifth classes are much smaller and the fifth class is of frosted silver instead of white enamel. They are worn on the left side of the coat with other medals.

The Most Excellent Order of the British Empire

This Order was founded by King George V in 1917 as an Order in five classes open to both men and women alike. In 1918 a military division was instituted and designated by a central stripe running down the centre of the riband.

There is also a medal of the Order designated The British Empire Medal. This Order is of wider application than any of the other Orders of Chivalry and admissions to the Order are made for any exceptional or valuable services.

Between the 1st January, 1958 and the 20th June, 1974 admissions to the Order and awards of the Medal in respect of gallantry were distinguished from those for meritorious service by the wording of the publication in the London Gazette and by the wearing of a silver emblem of two crossed oak leaves on the appropriate riband. With the institution in June, 1974 of the Queen's Gallantry Medal it was ordered that no further admissions to the Order or awards of the Medal for gallantry would be made.

The original purple riband was replaced in 1935 by one of rose-pink edged with two stripes of pearl-grey. The riband of the military division is denoted by a further central stripe of pearl-grey .

The five classes of this Order are as follows:

    Knights or Dames Grand Cross, (G.B.E.).
    Knights or Dames Commanders, (K. or D.B.E.).
    Commanders, (C.B.E.).
    Officers, (O.B.E.).
    Members, (M.B.E.).

The mantle for Knights and Dames Grand Cross is of rose-pink satin lined with pearl-grey silk and there is a gold Collar. Insignia for all classes are worn in a similar manner to those of the Royal Victorian Order; the Badge of an Officer being smaller than that of a Commander and made of silver gilt and the Badge of a Member being similar to that of an Officer except that it is made of silver.

29

The Order of Merit and the Order of the Companions of Honour

THE ORDER OF MERIT was founded by King Edward VII on the 23rd June, 1902 and like the appointments to the Royal Victorian Order, is a personal award from the Sovereign. The Order carries no title or rank and is of one class only although the badge itself differs when awarded for military service. It is one of the most coveted of all distinctions.

The establishment is limited to twenty-four, other than honorary members, and the Order is awarded for outstanding services in the armed services or for services in art, literature or science.

Our illustration shows the badge for civil services, those for military services being distinguished by the addition of two silver swords with gold hilts placed saltire-wise between the angles of the cross. The badge is worn from a riband, half blue and half crimson, around the neck. The first woman to be admitted to the Order was Miss Florence Nightingale.

THE COMPANIONS OF HONOUR. This Order was founded by King George V in 1917.

The Order is limited in number, male or female, to sixty-five. Appointments to the Order are made on the recommendation of the Prime Minister and foreign citizens may be appointed as honorary members. Appointments are made to persons who have rendered conspicuous service of national importance. There is only one class and the badge is worn suspended from a riband of carmine with borders of gold thread from around the neck in the case of men and on the left side of the dress suspended from a riband in the form of a bow for ladies.

Imperial Service Order

This Order and the medal of the Order were instituted by King Edward VII in 1902. The Order, which is of one class only, is open to both male and female members of the Civil Service both at home and overseas. The medal is awarded to more junior ranks of the Civil Service who do not qualify for Companionship of the Order. Companions of the Order use the post nominal letters I.S.O. The insignia is different for men and women and is worn by men from the left breast with other medals and by women on a bow from the left shoulder. The insignia for men consists of a gold plaque in the centre of which is the royal cypher with the words "For Faithful Service" around it in blue lettering, the whole surrounded by a seven pointed star which in the case of the insignia for women becomes a silver laurel wreath.

Admission to the Order is limited and is normally only given to those who have completed twenty-five years service, with correspondingly shorter periods for overseas service, but may be awarded to those who have given "eminently meritorious service" without condition as to length of service.

The medal to the Order was originally very similar to the Order but it is now of silver with the Sovereign's head on the obverse and with the same words "For Faithful Service" on the reverse. The recipient's name is engraved round the rim of the medal. Awards of the medal do not carry the right to use post-nominal letters.

Top: Imperial Service Medal for Ladies (old style).
Bottom: Imperial Service Order for Men

PART TWO

Decorations

Opposite: The 23rd, Royal Welch Fusiliers at
the Battle of Alma, Crimea War, 1854.
Detail from the painting by R. Simpkin, courtesy of National Army Museum.

Obverse

The Victoria Cross

Founded by Queen Victoria in 1856, this is the highest award which may be given for gallantry in the face of the enemy. It may only be awarded to members of the services and is open to both men and women, though no woman has, as yet, received it. Since its foundation there have been nearly 1,400 awards. Bars may be awarded for additional acts of gallantry which would otherwise have merited the award of the Cross and there have been three awards of a Bar to: Lieut. A. M. Martin-Leake, R.A.M.C., (V.C. 1902: Bar 1914). Capt. N. G. Chevasse, R.A.M.C., (V.C. 1916: Bar 1917 posthumous). Capt. C. H. Upham (New Zealand Forces), V.C. 1941: Bar 1942).

The crosses, which are cast by hand by Messrs. Hancocks of London, are still made from the metal of the guns captured at the siege of Sebastopol.

The first Cross was awarded to Mate C. D. Lucas R.N. for his action in throwing a live bomb overboard from his ship in June 1854 during the Crimea War. The most recent winner was W.O. II Keith Payne, Australian Army Training Team, in May 1969 in Vietnam. Under Clause 13 of the Warrant, where more than 50 men take part in an action, the officers, W.O's and N.C.O's, and the other Ranks may each choose amongst themselves a candidate for the award of the Cross. The youngest recipient was Hospital Apprentice A. Fitzgibbon of the Indian Hospital Administration who was 15 years 3 months when he won his Cross at the Taku Forts in 1860; the oldest, Capt. W. Raynor, Bengal Veteran Establishment, who was about 69 when he won his Cross in the Indian Mutiny.

The ribbon was originally blue for the Royal Navy and crimson for the Army until 1920 when it was changed to crimson for all Services.

Obverse

The George Cross

Founded by King George VI in 1940 as the highest award for acts of con-spicuous gallantry performed by men or women when not in the face of the enemy. In order of precedence it comes immediately after the V.C. because of its newer foundation but before all other Orders or decorations. Bars may be won for additional acts of gallantry but to date no such awards have been made. At the time of its inception, living recipients of the Empire Gallantry Medal should have exchanged their medals for the George Cross and the Empire Gallantry Medal then became obsolete. In 1971 surviving holders of the Albert Medal and Edward Medals were also enabled to exchange their medals for the George Cross. Apart from these exchanges there have been nearly 150 recipients of the Cross, of which six have been women (two of the latter were exchange E.G.M.).

In April 1942 King George VI awarded the Maltese Islands the Cross in recognition of the gallantry of the inhabitants during the intense bombard-ment of the islands from 1940 to 1943. The youngest recipient of the Cross is John Bamford who won it at the age of 15 years in 1952 as a colliery worker. The oldest recipient is John Ascon an engine driver, who was 57 years old when he won his Cross on the 9th February, 1957.

As with the Victoria Cross, all living recipients receive a tax free annuity of £100. Both the V.C. and the G.C. may be awarded posthumously and so high is the standard of courage required before an award is made that many of them are.

Obverse

Distinguished Service Order

Founded in 1886 by Queen Victoria. Appointments as Companions of the Distinguished Service Order are made to officers of the three armed services for gallantry or for distinguished service in the face of the enemy.

In 1943 a new Warrant extended elegibility to officers of the Merchant Navy, although the first of such awards were gazetted in September, 1942.

Although strictly speaking an Order it has been thought more convenient to place it within this section.

In 1916 an amendment to the Warrant allowed for the award of bars for subsequent acts of gallantry and to date 17 third bars have been awarded, 7 of them during the First World War, 8 during the Second World War and 1 during the Korean War. Since its inception nearly 17,000 initial awards have been made.

Officers awarded the D.S.O., particularly those of the rank of Captain or below in the Army, or equivalent rank in the other services, have often just "missed" the award of the V.C.

Apart from the change in the Royal Cypher, this medal has changed very little since 1886, and is one of the most attractive of all medals.

Obverse

Royal Red Cross

Founded in 1883 by Queen Victoria, this decoration is in two classes. Thoses awarded the First Class are designated "Members": those awarded the Second Class are designated "Associates". The post nominal letters are R.R.C. and A.R.R.C. respectively. The award is confined to ladies in the Nursing Services or ladies who have given outstanding service in the care of the sick or wounded of the fighting services.

There is provision for the grant of second award bars to the First Class, and for promotion from the Second to the First Class.

The badge of either class is worn suspended from a bow on the left shoulder. It has been said that the suggestion for the founding of this decoration was made to Queen Victoria by Miss Florence Nightingale.

Distinguished Service Cross

Obverse

Founded by King Edward VII as the Conspicuous Service Cross it was changed and given its present name in 1914. The Cross is for award to Officers of the Royal Navy up to and including the rank of Commander, for acts of gallantry in the face of the enemy. Bars may be awarded for further acts of gallantry.

Provision is made for officers of equivalent rank in the Royal Marines, the Army, R.A.F. and Merchant Navy to be eligible when serving afloat. Only eight awards were made of the C.S.C. before the change of name. Bars for subsequent acts were authorized in 1916 and one third bar has been awarded (Cdr. N. E. Morley R.N.V.R. in 1945). Approximately 1,700 Crosses were awarded in World War I and 4,500 Crosses were awarded in World War II.

Military Cross

Obverse

Founded in 1914 by King George V for gallant and distinguished service in action by officers in the Army of the rank of Captain or below and Warrant Officers. Bars were authorized for additional acts of gallantry by Warrant in 1916. Further amendments in 1917, 1918, 1920, 1931 and 1953 allowed the award to officers of equivalent rank in the other services when operating on the ground and allowed awards to substantive Majors. There have been four awards of a third bar, all in the First World War, when 37,031 Crosses and 3,123 Bars in total were awarded. During the Second World War the numbers were 10,386 Crosses and 506 Bars. Approximately 600 Crosses have been awarded since the last World War which gives an indication of the number of actions in which the British Army and Dominion Armies have been engaged since that time.

Distinguished Flying Cross

Obverse

Founded by King George V in 1918 on the formation of the Royal Air Force for gallantry in action whilst engaged in flying operations against the enemy by Officers and Warrant Officers. Provision was made for the award of bars for additional acts of valour. Prior to the institution of the R.A.F., pilots in the R.F.C. were awarded the M.C. in similar circumstances. Subsequent Warrants extended the award to the Fleet Air Arm, the Royal Marines and to those in the other services who fly (e.g. Glider Regiment pilots). The original ribbon of the D.F.C. had the stripes running horizontally, but this was changed to the present ribbon in 1919. Only just over 1,000 Crosses were awarded for the 1914–18 War and they are therefore rare. During the 1939–45 War, however, with the enormous expansion of the Service and many actions, the number of Crosses and bars was 20,946.

Air Force Cross

Obverse

Founded by King George V in December, 1918, the Cross is a reward for outstanding services or acts of outstanding courage in the air when not on active service against an enemy. It may be awarded, in addition to officers and warrant officers of the R.A.F., to Naval, Military or Civil personnel who render similar service whilst flying. Provision is made for the award of bars for subsequent acts which would have gained the award of the Cross.

Like the D.F.C. the ribbon was originally with horizontal stripes which were changed in 1919 to the present design. It is unusual to find a citation for the award of this Cross in the London Gazette, but in fact the award of this decoration marks the display of courage under unusual and varying circumstances and flying skill of the highest order.

PART THREE

Medals for Gallantry and Distinguished Conduct

Opposite: Rocket-firing Typhoons attacking German armoured
formations at the Battle of the Falaise Gap, Normandy, 1944.
Detail from the painting by Frank Wootton, courtesy of the Imperial War Museum.

Obverse

The Albert Medal

Founded by Queen Victoria in 1866 in memory of her late husband. This award was made for acts of gallantry on land or sea. It is no longer awarded because of the founding of the George Cross and George Medal. There are gold and bronze medals which differ slightly when awarded for action on land or sea. The illustration shows the bronze Albert Medal for land. When awarded for land the riband is as illustrated, when awarded for sea the red stripes are in blue.

Medals awarded in gold were known as the Albert Medal First Class; those in bronze, the Albert Medal Second Class. In November, 1949 King George VI, because of the foundation of the George Cross and George Medal, gave approval that the award of gold medals should cease and those in bronze should only be awarded posthumously. In 1971 H.M. The Queen ordered that all living recipients of the Albert Medal both in gold and bronze should exchange their medals for the George Cross at a special investiture. Recipients were entitled to use the post-nominal letters A.M. and from 1968 received the £100 annuity given to holders of the V.C. and G.C.

The inscription on the back of each medal is unusually long and gives more detail of the act than most gallantry awards.

From 1866 to 1969 a total of 69 in gold and 491 in bronze were awarded.

Distinguished Conduct Medal

Founded by Queen Victoria in 1854. The Distinguished Conduct Medal is awarded for acts of gallantry which, though conspicuous, do not merit the award of the Victoria Cross. It is open to Warrant Officers, Non-Commissioned Officers and men of the Army.

It may also be awarded to men of the Royal Navy, the Royal Marines and the Royal Air Force when the act of gallantry is performed on land.

Bars may be awarded for subsequent acts of gallantry and 11 second bars have been awarded since 1881 when bars were first authorised.

During the 1914–18 War 24,571 D.C.M's, 469 first bars and 10 second bars were awarded. However, in common with many gallantry awards, the number awarded in World War II was much smaller, being 1,879 and 19 first bars.

Obverse

Conspicuous Gallantry Medal

Founded originally in 1855 for gallantry by Petty Officers and men of the Royal Navy and Sergeants and men of the Royal Marines, this medal was discontinued after the Crimean War.

In 1874 the medal was revived for award to Petty Officers and men of the Royal Navy and Sergeants and men of the Royal Marines for conspicuous acts of gallantry which did not merit the award of the Victoria Cross. Bars may be given for further acts of gallantry though only one bar has been awarded (Chief Petty Officer A. R. Blore, in 1918). In 1943 King George VI created the Conspicuous Gallantry Medal (Flying) for Warrant Officers, Non-Commissioned Officers and airmen of the Royal Air Force, which has a different riband.

The C.G.M. is one of the rarest awards to the services, there being only 108 during the 1914–18 War, 72 during the 1939–45 War and 103 C.G.M's (Flying) from 1943 to 1945.

Reverse

George Medal

Reverse

The George Medal was founded by King George VI in 1940, at the same time as the George Cross. The circumstances of award are exactly the same as those of the George Cross except that the act of gallantry for which the award is made need not be of such a high order as that which would merit the award of the Cross. Bars for additional acts of gallantry may be awarded and to date twenty-five such bars have been won.

Lt. Hugh Randall Syme R.A.N.V.R. was awarded a bar to his G.M. and the George Cross as well. Four other recipients of the George Cross also hold the George Medal. The year of the award of a bar is engraved on the reverse.

Queen's Police Medal, Queen's Fire Services Medal

Reverse

Founded originally in 1909 as the King's Police Medal, awards were made for both gallantry and distinguished service, the reverse of the medal being different in either case. It can be awarded to members of the Police or of the Fire Services. The ribbon when awarded for gallantry has an additional red stripe through each white stripe. In 1940 the name of the medal changed to the King's Police and Fire Services Medal and after 1949 those awarded for gallantry were posthumous. In 1954 two new medals were created, one for each service, known as the Queen's Police Medal and the Queen's Fire Services Medal, but again award of either medal for gallantry is posthumous. Where members of either service perform a gallant act and survive they are awarded the G.C., the G.M., or the B.E.M. for Gallantry. It is difficult to understand why the gallantry divisions of the Q.P.M. and Q.F.S.M. are not discontinued.

Edward Medal

Founded by King Edward VII to reward acts of gallantry in mines and quarries, the medal was originally in two classes, the First in silver the Second in bronze. Provision was made for the award of bars for subsequent acts of heroism. In 1909 a new Warrant increased the scope of the award to industry in general and provided two reverses to the medal, one for mines and one for industry. In 1917 the name of the Medal was changed to The Edward Medal in Silver and The Edward Medal, the second of which continued to be struck in bronze. In 1949 King George VI made similar regulations to those he had made for the Albert Medal because of the existence of the G.C. and G.M. In all, 102 medals in silver and 481 in bronze and 2 bars were awarded. In 1971 surviving holders of the Edward Medal, like those of the Albert Medal, exchanged their medals for the George Cross.

Obverse

Distinguished Service Medal

Founded by King George V in October 1914 as a junior award to the Conspicuous Gallantry Medal for acts of gallantry by Petty Officers and men of the Royal Navy and N.C.O's and men of the Royal Marines. It may also be awarded to men of equivalent rank in the other two services and the Merchant Navy, when serving afloat. Bars, authorized in 1916, were dated during World War I but undated thereafter. There has been one three bar medal to Temp. Petty Officer W. H. Kelly in 1944. Approximately 5,500 medals in World War I and approximately 7,700 medals in World War II were awarded. Several awards have been made to members of the Royal Australian Navy during the war in Vietnam.

Reverse

Reverse

Military Medal

Although founded by King George V in 1916 for award to N.C.O's and other ranks in the Army for "Bravery in the Field", the first awards dated back to the beginning of the 1914–1918 War. Provision was made for the award of bars. Subsequent Warrants extended the award to women and to Warrant Officers, as well as to personnel in the other services when operating on the ground. Well over 100 awards of this medal have been made to women for bravery under fire. One third bar was awarded to Corporal E. A. Corey of the Australian Infantry in the London Gazette of 17th June, 1919.

During the dreadful fighting of 1914–18 no less than 120,000 M.M's and bars were awarded. In the period 1939–45 the number was 15, 491. As with the M.C. many have been awarded since 1945 in the many overseas actions in which the Armies of the Commonwealth have been engaged.

Reverse

Distinguished Flying Medal

Founded by King George V in 1918 under almost the same conditions as the D.F.C. except that it is for award to N.C.O's and men of the R.A.F. or other services whilst engaged in flying operations against the enemy. Originally designed with the stripes on the ribbon being horizontal they were changed to the present ribbon in 1919. Because fewer N.C.O's fly than officers the Medal is much rarer than the Cross. Just over 100 Medals and bars were awarded during the 1914–1918 War and 6,698 in World War II. One second bar was awarded to Flight Sgt. D. E. Kingaby R.A.F.V.R. in 1941. He was subsequently commissioned and awarded both the D.S.O. and D.F.C.

Air Force Medal

Founded by King George V in 1918 and awarded under the same circumstances as the Air Force Cross, to N.C.O's and men of the R.A.F. as well as to others engaged in flying operations not in action against an enemy. Bars may be awarded for further services or acts.

The Air Force Medal is extremely rare, there having been just over 800 awarded since its inception, with 7 bars. Like the A.F.C. the original ribbon had horizontal stripes, changed to the present design in 1919.

Reverse

Queen's Gallantry Medal

On the 20th June, 1974 Her Majesty the Queen instituted a new Medal for Gallantry as a junior award to the George Medal, designed to reward exemplary acts of bravery under similar conditions to those which would previously have earned the British Empire Medal for Gallantry or membership of the Order of the British Empire for Gallantry. It replaces those awards, and awards of the British Empire Medal and membership of the Order of the British Empire will in future only be made for distinguished service. Recipients are entitled to the post nominal letters Q.G.M. and bars may be awarded for further acts of bravery which would otherwise have earned the medal.

Reverse

PART FOUR

Campaign Medals

Opposite: Admiral Beatty's flagship, the Battle-Cruiser *Lion*,
in action at the Battle of the Dogger Bank, 1915.
Detail from the painting by Arthur Burgess, courtesy of the Imperial War Museum.

Obverse

Naval Gold Medals

These medals were instituted in 1795 and were issued until 1815. Basically they are of the same design except that the reverses are slightly different. Reverses on both are engraved with rank, name of recipient, battle and date for which award was given but, in the case of the Large Medal, these details are surrounded by a wreath of oak and laurel leaves. The Large Medal is two inches in diameter and the small medal 1.3 inches. Both medals are fitted in gold frames, glazed on both sides.

22 large medals were awarded and 177 of the smaller.

The actions for which these medals were awarded are:– 1st June, 1794; St. Vincent, 1797; Camperdown, 1797; Nile, 1798; Recapture of Hermione, 1799; Trafalgar, 1805; 4th November, 1805; St. Domingo, 1806; Curacoa, 1807; Capture of Thetis, 1808; Capture of Badere Zaffer, 1808; Capture of Furieuse, 1809; Lissa, 1811; Banda Neira, 1811; 'Capture of Rivoli, 1812; Capture of

Chesapeake, 1813; Capture of L'Etoile, 1814; Endymion with President, 1815.

Admirals and Captains were awarded these medals and, also, those who survived to submit claims were entitled to the Naval General Service, with bar for the same action as their gold medal.

From the number issued it will be seen that these medals are extremely rare, and it would be necessary to go back a good number of years to find when a Large Naval Gold Medal was sold by auction. The Small Naval Gold Medal awarded to Admiral Sir Pulteney Malcolm for the Battle of St. Domingo was sold at Glendining's on 21st April 1971 and realised £1,100. This medal was in a group which included a breast star of the Order of the Bath and collar and breast star of the Order of St. Michael and St. George.

Bars were not awarded and officers such as Nelson and Collingwood received more than one medal.

Army Gold Crosses

The London Gazette of 7th October 1813 gives full information on the award of these crosses but it is too lengthy to quote within the scope of this work. Prior to their award a recipient must have participated in three battles, for which he would have received a gold medal with two bars. On taking part in a fourth battle the medal was substituted by a cross, which had the names of the battles, struck in relief, for which the cross was granted. Bars were granted for any further actions, and the Duke of Wellington received a cross with nine bars. Details of recipient were engraved on the edges of the cross. 163 crosses were awarded and, although much rarer, of recent years they have often sold at public auction for less than some Victoria Crosses. At Glendining's in December 1969 a Gold Cross to Lt. Col. Charles Fox Canning, together with his small Army Gold medal and Waterloo medal, sold for £2,500.00.

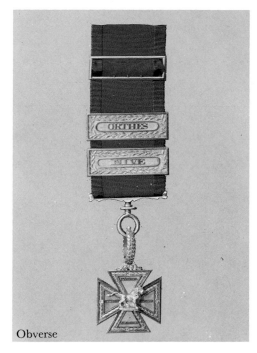

Obverse

Army Gold Medals

Full information on the award of these medals is given in the same London Gazette referred to when giving details of the Army Gold Cross and, as mentioned then, a recipient could receive a maximum of two bars, having participated in three battles. The battles they commemorated were the same as those on the MGS 1793–1814. Generals received the large medal whilst the small was mainly awarded to Majors and above. There are exceptions, as the criterion seems to have been that a recipient had to be in command. Both types are fitted in gold frames, which have details of recipient engraved on them, usually at the bottom, but examples have been seen, on the smaller medals, where the naming is engraved at the top, on either side of the suspender.

The name of the battle is engraved on the reverse, but those who qualified for Roleia and Vimiera seem to have received the one medal with these actions engraved on it. For Barrosa the name of the battle was struck, in relief. A special medal was struck for Maida.

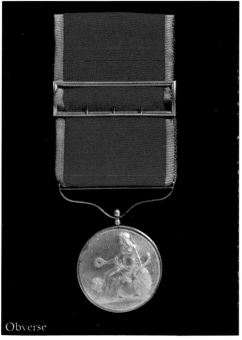

Obverse

Reverse

Naval General Service
Medal

1793–1840

As with its military equivalent, being issued in 1849, this medal mainly commemorates battles and engagements that had taken place many years earlier, although the bars are consistent with the period covered; the first being Nymphe 18th June, 1793 and the last for Syria (November 1840). In common with the Military General Service medal it was only forwarded to survivors who submitted claims. The date 1848, which appears on the obverse, below the diademed head of Queen Victoria, is the year in which a list was published of actions qualifying for bars.

The total of bars authorised was two hundred and thirty one, and it is impossible, therefore, within the scope of this book, to list them. They were awarded for fleet actions such as Lord Howe's famous victory on 1st June, 1794, Camperdown (11th October, 1797) and, as is to be expected, all Nelson's victories – Nile (1st August, 1798), Copenhagen (2nd April, 1801) and Trafalgar (21st October, 1805).

Ship versus ship actions were also recognised, an outstanding example being the well known engagement between HMS Shannon and the American frigate Chesapeake, which was fought outside Boston Harbour on 1st June, 1813. Many of the services carried out by boats from ships were rewarded by what are termed Boat Service bars. These had the words "Boat Service" struck in relief, as with all other bars, between the date, which is engraved. An example is 14 Dec (engraved) Boat Service (in relief) 1814 (engraved). These boat service actions total fifty five. Unpublished but nevertheless genuine bars are also known. All told some 24,000 medals were issued but this figure must be regarded as approximate.

The maximum number of bars gained on any one medal was seven, and three such are now known. One of these, the medal to Gunner Thomas Haines, was sold at Sotheby's in January 1972, for £1,600.00, which is the highest known price for a Naval General Service Medal. This particular medal warrants a special note as, prior to it appearing at Sotheby's, only two seven bar N.G.S. were recorded. It must also be unique in that, despite having one rank removed and another unofficially engraved, with one bar not in the correct order of sequence and two others unconfirmed by the medal roll, a record price was still established. With many present day collectors tending to be perfectionists this is somewhat surprising, but the eventual owner has obviously made a true study of his hobby, realising medals can be subject to imperfections and that rolls do not always provide conclusive evidence of a medal being genuine.

It is possible for the unscrupulous to remove a bar from a common medal such as Syria (over 7,000 issued) and add that of a rare issue where the name is the same on each roll. A good example would be the medal to John Jones who appears on the roll for the bar "Crescent 20 Octr. 1793" (12 issued) and twelve of the same name were entitled to Syria. One has to take into account that until comparatively recent years prices remained unchanged, and the NGS and MGS were virtually the only medals worth the attention of the forger.

Military General Service Medal
1793—1814

This medal was authorised by General Order dated 1st June, 1847 and mainly commemorates the battles of the Napoleonic Wars. There are several anomalies, such as the reverse bearing the dates 1793–1814 when the earliest bar on the medal was for Egypt 1801, and the obverse bears the date 1848 the year of issue. Being instituted during her reign it carries the head of Queen Victoria who, of course, was not even born at the time of some of the earlier battles for which bars were awarded for.

Only survivors who had submitted claims received the medal, hence the comparatively limited number of approximately 26,000; but it was also forwarded to the next-of-kin of claimants who had died prior to distribution. The 29 bars issued are as listed and, in keeping with the anomalies already mentioned, the Egypt bar, although for the earliest action, was the last to be authorised in 1850.

Egypt (2.3.1801 to 2.9.1801); Maida (4.7.1806); Roleia (17.8.1808); Vimiera (21.8.1808); Sahagun (21.12.1808); Benevente (29.12.1808); Sahagun and Benevente (Awarded to those present at both actions); Corunna (16.1.1809); Martinique (30.1.1809 to 24.2.1809); Talavera (27/28.7.1809); Guadaloupe (Jan./Feb. 1810); Busaco (27.9.1810); Barrosa (5.4.1811); Fuentes D'Onor (5.5.1811); Albuhera (16.5.1811); Java (10.8.1811 to 26.8.1811); Ciudad Rodrigo (8.1.1812 to 19.1.1812); Badajoz (17.3.1812 to 6.4.1812); Salamanca (22.7.1812); Fort Detroit (Aug. 1812); Vittoria (21.6.1813); Pyrenees (25.7.1813 to 2.8.1813); St. Sebastian (17.7.1813 to 8.7.1813); Chateauguay (26.10.1813); Nivelle (10.11.1813); Chrystler's Farm (11.11.1813); Nive (9.12.1813 to 13.12.1813); Orthes (27.2.1814); Toulouse (10.4.1814).

Reverse

The medal was never issued without at least one bar and the recipient's initial (sometimes Christian name) surname and regiment are impressed in small serif lettering on the rim. In the case of officers and non-commissioned officers the rank is also given.

Two recipients received the medal with 15 bars and those with 14 bars are also of the highest rarity.

The rarest bar is for Benevente of which only 10 were awarded. The highest recorded auction price for a Military General Service Medal is £950. This was with bars for Fort Detroit, Chateauguary and Chrystler's Farm awarded to J. B. Lapierre, Canadian Militia, and is the only one with these three bars. It was sold by Glendining's in December 1965.

Obverse

Seringapatam Medal

17th April—4th May 1799

There are two strikings of this medal as it was made at the Birmingham Mint and Calcutta Mint. The English one measures 1.9 inches and the Calcutta issue 1.8 inches. The first mentioned was struck in gold, silver, bronze and tin, and silver gilt medals are also known. The Calcutta Mint made them in gold and silver.

Apart from the difference in the sizes, the English and Calcutta medals can be distinguished by the designer's initials, which are found on the right of the reverse, just above the exergue. On the English strikings the initials are C.H.K., whilst for the Calcutta one these are in a different order and the K is reversed; thus C.Я.H.

The Seringapatam medals were issued without means of suspension, as they were apparently meant to be commemorative medallions, but they were worn, and are found with various fitments subsequently added.

Reverse

Waterloo Medal

1815

In addition to commemorating what was possibly the greatest land battle fought by Britain during the 19th century, this has the distinction of being the first campaign medal issued by the British Government to all officers and men, including those regiments in reserve and, also, to the various units of the King's German Legion. Unlike the Military General Service it was also sent to the next-of-kin of men killed.

The naming is in large impressed Roman capitals, and in order to read the inscription on the rim it is necessary to have the reverse facing. A 'Star' is nearly always included at each end of the naming and it would be unusual to find a genuine medal without these.

At Glendining's auction of February 1963 the medal to a Sergeant Major of the 6th Inniskilling Dragoons realised £210.00. This is possibly the highest price recorded for a Waterloo Medal awarded to an other rank.

Burmah Medal,

1824—1826

The Honourable East India Company sanctioned this medal in April 1826 as an award to native officers and troops who served in the war in Ava, as it is generally called, and for which British regiments received the Army of India medal, 1799–1826, with Ava bar.

Officers and officials received gold medals and soldiers had theirs in silver. Although not normally given to British personnel a few officers may have been presented with gold medals, and one is known to be in the group of orders and medals awarded to Sir Willoughby Cotton.

All medals were issued unnamed and it would be most unusual to find one which had been privately named.

In common with several others of the earlier period the suspension of this medal was by means of a steel clip, clamped to the piece, through which passed either a ring or straight bar suspender.

Reverse

Army of India Medal

1799—1826

This was instituted in 1851 and is yet another instance of a medal being awarded to survivors of battles which had been fought many years previously.

The following twenty one bars were authorised:–
Allighur, Battle of Delhi, Assye, Asseerghur, Laswarree, Argaum, Gawilghur, Defence of Delhi, Battle of Deig, Capture of Deig, Nepaul, Kirkee, Poona, Kirkee and Poona, Seetabuldee, Nagpore, Seetabuldee & Nagpore, Maheidpoor, Corygaum, Ava, Bhurtpoor.

Naming is usually in small impressed serif capitals but those to the Indian Army are often engraved in running script or rather uneven and somewhat more heavily impressed serif capitals. Seven bars was the greatest number issued on one medal and only one was awarded. A medal with six bars to Major J. Greenstreet, 2/15th N.I. realised £650 when sold by Glendinings on 17th December, 1969.

Reverse

Obverse

Ghuznee Medal

1839

Awarded to those who took part in the capture of the fortress of Ghuznee, 21st–23rd July 1839, this medal was struck at the Calcutta Mint.

Although issued unnamed, many medals are found engraved in various styles, either on the reverse, in the field, or on the rim. Impressed naming is found on some medals. It would seem certain that some regiments were responsible for naming the medals issued to them.

In addition to the Calcutta Mint striking there is another type which is of somewhat superior finish, with the detail in much higher relief. This could be a British made copy and, does not carry the initials of the designer, which are to be found on the reverse of the original.

One reference book states that only two hundred and thirty nine medals were issued to Europeans. This is obviously a misprint as two British cavalry and four infantry regiments were engaged in the capture of this fortress.

Obverse

Jellalabad Medals

1841—1842

There are two types of this medal and they are generally referred to as Mural Crown, and Flying Victory, the descriptions applying to the obverse of the first mentioned and to the reverse of the other. The Mural Crown issue, which was minted in Calcutta, was considered unsuitable so another medal was struck in London with the diademed head of Queen Victoria and legend "Victoria Vindex" on the obverse. A few had "Victoria Regina". Those who had received the Mural Crown type were supposed to exchange them for the new issue but the numbers who did so seem uncertain.

The 13th Light Infantry were the main British troops who defended Jellalabad and medals to them are generally considered to be the most desirable. For its distinguished gallantry during campaigns in Burma and Afghanistan Queen Victoria granted the title of 13th Prince Albert's Light Infantry to the regiment and the battle honour "Jellalabad".

First Afghan War Medals

1839—1842

Altogether seven medals were struck for this war, including Ghuznee 1839, Jellalabad and Kelat-I-Ghilzie which are all described separately.

Also there are obverse variations such as "Victoria Regina" legend instead of "Victoria Vindex". In the case of the issue for Cabul a few were spelt Cabvl. Additionally there are the two medals for Jellalabad.

The four types now dealt with are as under: Candahar (May 1842), Cabul (15th September 1842), Ghuznee-Cabul, Candahar-Ghuznee-Cabul.

Except for Cabul, all these medals are scarce to British troops and those for Candahar and Ghuznee-Cabul are quite rare.

All types were issued unnamed but of those that were later engraved the most common style is in running script. Medals to the 41st Regiment, however, are usually engraved in capitals.

Reverse

Kelat-I-Ghilzie Medal

1842

Awarded for the defence of the fort, from which the medal received its name, this is one of the rarer British campaign medals, especially to European recipients, as the garrison consisted of mainly Indian troops.

The naming is in the usual running script, but several varieties of this have been noted and, as all these medals appear to have been originally issued unnamed, those that are named required careful scrutiny. It is usually possible to discern Indian style engraving but to do so requires experience which can only be gained by handling medals.

A roll of those who served with 4th Company 2nd Battalion Bengal Artillery exists by which it is possible to verify medals to this unit.

In the later part of 1971 a London dealer had a medal to the 43rd Bengal R.I. priced at £160.00 but, with the number of collectors growing steadily each month, there has been an overall increase in prices since then.

Reverse

Reverse

Scinde Campaign Medals

1843

As detailed below, there are three different reverses to this medal, which was authorised in September 1843.

Meeanee (17th February 1843), Hyderabad (24th March 1843), Meeanee-Hyderabad (1843).

They are all rare and "Meeanee" could be classified as very rare, especially to the 22nd Regiment, who greatly distinguished themselves, being the only British infantry battalion present during this campaign. Medals to them are the most prized by collectors. A roll is readily available to this regiment for the purpose of verification.

A flotilla from the Indian Navy, consisting of "Comet", "Meteor", "Nimrod", "Planet" and "Satellite" were also present and qualified for either Meeanee or Hyderabad, but medals to them are very rare.

Obverse

Gwalior Campaign Stars

1843

These bronze stars were authorised by a General Order of January 1844 and the metal is said to have been from captured enemy guns. They were awarded for the battles of Punniar and Maharajpoor, both of which were fought on the same day—29th December 1843. The centre of these stars consists of a smaller silver star on which is the name of the battle and the date mentioned above.

Originally, it would appear that they were not intended to be worn from a ribbon, as they were issued with just a brass hook on the reverse, but they are usually seen with either a straight suspender or large ring attached to the hook for the ribbon to be fitted.

They are scarce to British troops as only the 16th Lancers, 39th and 40th regiments were at Maharajpoor and the 9th Lancers, 3rd and 50th Regiments at Punniar. British Artillerymen were also present.

China Medal

1842

This medal was authorised in 1843 and was awarded to British and Indian regiments, together with ships from the Royal Navy and East India Company.

Incredible as it may seem today the war was caused because the British merchants wished to import opium from India, whereas the Chinese Government would not allow this, and refused to pay compensation after burning huge stocks of the drug.

The naming is exactly the same style as on the Waterloo medal, and is again read with the reverse facing.

The China 1842 was the first campaign medal to be issued with the head of Queen Victoria. No bars were authorised.

The first design for this medal depicted, on the reverse, a lion with its forepaws on a dragon. Examples are occasionally seen, unnamed, and are quite rare.

Reverse

Sutlej Medal

1845—1846

Sanction for this medal was given by a General Order of 17th April 1846 and, although four battles are commemorated, only three bars are possible on any one medal. This was because the first battle in which a recipient took part is named in the exergue. This does not occur on any other British campaign medal and, also, the Sutlej was the first instance of bars being awarded.

The four battles were Moodkee, Ferozeshuhur, Aliwal and Sobraon, with bars being issued for all but the first mentioned.

Two British regiments, the 31st and 50th were engaged in all these battles and medals to them, with three bars, are very much sought after.

The present selling price of a medal with three bars is in the region of sixty to seventy pounds and, as most dealers hold rolls for the 31st and 50th regiments, it is usually easy to verify any such medals.

Reverse

Reverse

New Zealand Medal
1845—1847, 1860—1866

Medals for both campaigns against the Maoris were sanctioned in 1869 and, taking into account that there are at least twenty nine varieties of dates recorded, plus undated issues, it is probably the most complex of all the British campaign series. Some dates are extremely rare, whilst even the more common can be rare to a regiment.

For the 1845–1847 campaign the Army received undated medals, although a dated one to the commanding officer of the 65th Regiment is stated to be in a museum. As the 65th Regiment served in both wars and it is possible to get undated medals for either, it is necessary to refer to a medal roll to verify in which campaign a recipient took part. Undated medals to the Army for the earlier war are scarce, and to the 96th and 99th regiments they can be classified as rare, especially the first mentioned.

Reverse

Punjab Medal
1848—1849

The award of this medal was for the second war against the Sikhs, the first being the Sutlej campaign of 1845–1846 and, with this issue, three bars were authorised. These were for Mooltan, Chilianwala and Goojerat. The maximum number of bars on one medal is two, being either a combination of Chilianwala and Goojerat or Mooltan and Goojerat. This medal was also issued without bars.

At the battle of Chilianwala, 13th January, 1849, the 24th Regiment suffered severely, incurring losses of twenty one officers and over five hundred men. Medals to those killed in action at this disaster are greatly prized by collectors and, with perhaps the exception of one awarded to an officer with a distinguished record of service, the highest priced of this series. The last recorded auction price (September 1972) is fifty pounds. An officer casualty would obviously bring a higher price.

India General Service Medal

1854–1895

The original purpose of this medal, which was instituted in January 1854, was to commemorate the campaign that had taken place in Burma between March 1852 and June 1853. The bar for this was named Pegu, but allowances were made for further campaigns and, in all, twenty three bars, as listed below, were eventually authorised.

North West Frontier (Dec 1849–Oct 1868), Pegu (March 1852–June 1853), Persia (Dec 1856–Feb 1857), Umbeyla (Oct–Dec 1863), Bhootan (Dec 1864–Feb 1866) Looshai (Dec 1871–Feb 1872), Perak (Nov 1875–March 1876), Jowaki 1877–8 (Nov 1877–Jan 1878), Naga 1879–80 (Dec 1879–Jan 1880), Burma 1885–7 (Nov 1885–Apr 1887), Sikkim 1888 (March–Sept 1888), Hazara 1888 (Oct–Nov 1888), Burma 1887–89 (May 1887–Mar 1889), Chin Lushai 1889–90 (Nov 1889–Apr 1890), Samana 1891 (Apr–May 1891), Hazara 1891 (Mar–May 1891), N. E. Frontier 1891 (Mar–May 1891), Hunza 1891 (Dec. 1891), Burma 1889–92 (Apr 1889–Apr 1892), Lushai 1889–92 (Jan 1889–Jun 1892), Chin Hills 1892–93 (Oct. 1892–Mar 1893), Kachin Hills 1892–93 (Dec 1892–Mar 1893), Waziristan 1894–95 (Oct 1894–Mar 1895).

The rarest bars are Kachin Hills, Hunza 1891 and Chin Hills 1892–93. There were not any British regiments engaged in the Hunza campaign, and only a limited number from the Yorkshire Regiment took part in the expedition to the Kachin Hills. About two hundred men of the 1st Bn Norfolk Regiment received the Chin Hills bar. These latter medals are often found officially renamed and, as this bar was a retrospective award, it is practically certain that unclaimed medals, probably named to Indian recipients who had taken part in earlier campaigns, such as Burma 1885–7, had the naming removed and were then re-engraved. There are several different types of naming, the most common being in running script, but medals with the Pegu bar are indented in small serif capitals and those for Perak are engraved in sloping capitals. Other styles also apply to this medal, and

Reverse

more precise details can be found in Alec Purves's excellent book "Collecting Medals and Decorations".

The Royal Navy and Indian Navy had various ships and personnel present at several campaigns and could qualify for the following bars:– Pegu, Persia, Perak, Burma 1885–7. Indian Marine ships received the bar for Burma 1887–89. Native followers received medals in bronze and these started with the bar Burma 1885–7 and continued on India General Service medals until the reign of King George V. The final issue was for Abor 1911–12.

A medal to the Royal Navy with more than one bar would be definitely rare, and the same applies to a British Infantry regiment where a medal had more than two bars. In fact, in the latter instance, apart from a combination of "Burma" bars, any other two bars would be quite scarce.

A scarcer variation of the Burma 1887–89 bar is sometimes found, where the date reads 1887–9. An IGS 1854 with the date 1854 on the obverse is known to be in a collection.

Reverse

South Africa Medal

1834—1853

Instituted on November 1854 this medal was awarded for services in the Kaffir Wars of 1834–35, 1846–47 and 1850–53. No bars were authorised and some regiments took part in more than one of the campaigns and, in such cases, it is necessary to refer to a roll in order to establish a recipient's period of service.

The naming is in impressed serif capitals, which is standard to many earlier Victorian campaign medals. Army medals have initials, surname and regiment, but those to the Royal Navy bear only initials, name and rating. To find out on which ship a recipient served it is again necessary to consult a medal roll.

A table, giving numbers of medals issued to various regiments, including a breakdown for each campaign, is published in Major Gordon's "British Battles and Medals" (4th edition, revised by E. C. Joslin) but this is probably not complete.

Reverse

South Africa Medal

1877—1879

Authorised in 1880, this medal follows the pattern of the New Zealand issue for the Maori Wars of 1845–1860 and 1860–1866 in that it does not commemorate battles but a period of service.

Six bars were granted which carry the following dates: 1877, 1877–8, 1877–8–9, 1878, 1878–9, 1879. The 1877 bar is the rarest and those for 1877–8 and 1878 are very scarce on the market.

Although awarded for operations against various tribes, it is often referred to as the Zulu medal and, of course, the most famous events—Isandhlwana and Rorke's Drift—took place in this war. A medal to a recipient killed at Isandhlwana sells for about £150.00, and considerably more to one who had taken part in the defence of Rorke's Drift.

A few nurses received this medal and, according to one authority, also the 1879 bar, but it would seem almost certain they were awarded the medal only.

Crimea Medal

1854—1856

This medal, unlike those for earlier campaigns, was actually authorised while the war was still being fought and, in fact, many were distributed to troops still serving in the Crimea. Initially only bars for Alma (20th September, 1854) and Inkerman (5th November 1854) were sanctioned, hence just the date 1854 on the obverse, instead of dates covering the full period. Later, bars for Balaklava and Sebastopol were also awarded. Several regiments received all four bars, and it is also possible to get a medal without bar. Naval and Royal Marine personnel could receive the Azoff bar.

There are many varieties of naming found on this issue as, in addition to the small impressed serif capitals, which is the type classed as "official", it is known that some regiments carried out their own naming.

The most sought after medals are those where the recipient is known to have taken part in the charge of the Light Brigade. These usually sell for £150 or more.

Reverse

Baltic Medal

1854—1855

Approval for the issue of this medal was given on 23rd April 1856, after Queen Victoria's review of the Fleet at Spithead.

No bars were authorised and, to the Royal Navy, it was issued unnamed. Approximately one hundred of the Royal Sappers and Miners also qualified, and medals to them are named in the same type of impressed lettering already mentioned for the Crimea and other campaigns. It is of interest to note that medals to other ranks are named to Sappers and Miners, whilst those to officers are to the Royal Engineers. This is confirmed by the Baltic Medal issued to Capt. (Bt. Major) H. St. George Ord which, together with his K.C.M.G. and C.B. were in a London dealer's catalogue for December 1970 priced at £300.00.

There are two strikings of the Baltic medal, one being thicker. There are also differences in the claw fitment to the suspender.

Reverse

Reverse

Indian Mutiny Medal

1857—1858

Originally authorised in August 1868 to troops engaged against the mutineers, it was later extended to cover all persons who had borne arms or been under fire.

The following five bars were issued and, also, many gained the medal only. Delhi, Defence of Lucknow, Relief of Lucknow, Lucknow, Central India. Four bars is the maximum possible on any one medal and these are rare.

The most common naming is the small impressed serif capitals.

The Defence of Lucknow bar, when awarded to the original defenders (mainly the 32nd Light Infantry and some of the 84th Regiment) is in greatest demand, the last recorded auction price, for a medal to the 32nd L.I. being £80.00. Delhi also has great appeal as failure to capture this city would certainly have prolonged the campaign and might well have resulted in the loss of India.

Reverse

China Medal

1857—1860

The medal for the second China War was instituted in 1861 and the following six bars were authorised:–

China 1842, Fatshan 1857, Canton 1857, Taku Forts 1858, Taku Forts 1860, Pekin 1860.

Medals to the Royal Navy were issued unnamed, but those to the Indian Marine are found impressed in small serif style capitals, which also applies to the Army issues.

Because they are scarcer, medals to the 1st Dragoon Guards and 59th Regiment are the most sought after. The first mentioned were the only British cavalry regiment in the campaign and the 59th the only British regiment to gain the Canton 1857 bar. Those to the 44th and 67th Regiment are also desirable as, between them, they were awarded six Victoria Crosses for the attack on the Taku Forts, 21st August, 1860.

The rarest bar is China 1842 awarded to those who had been in the earlier war.

Canada General Service Medal

1866—1870

This provides yet another example of a medal being issued for a campaign that must have almost faded in the memory of many who had participated, as it was not authorised until January 1899.

The three undermentioned bars were issued, and there were a few recipients who gained all of them, including Sir Garnet Wolseley and Sir Redvers Buller.

Fenian Raid 1866, Fenian Raid 1870, Red River 1870.

The last mentioned is the rarest and, in December 1972, a medal with this single bar was on a dealer's list at £180.00. Fenian Raid 1870 is also quite scarce on the market, although some 4,500 single bars were issued.

In addition to the several British Army battalions, numerous Canadian units received the medal which is extremely rare to some of their volunteers and militia.

Reverse

Abyssinia Medal

1867—1868

This is said to be the most expensive general issue ever struck, on account of the naming, which is in embossed letters on the reverse. However, when issued to Indian troops the naming is often engraved in running script.

The expedition was under the command of General Sir Robert Napier, who later became Lord Napier of Magdala, and the forces employed came mainly from India.

The 3rd Dragoon Guards, 4th, 26th, 33rd, and 45th were the main British regiments, but detachments from others were also present. In this respect one reference work states that Lieut. D. du M. Gunton was the only recipient of the 96th Regiment. This is an error as the medal roll lists the following: 3 Officers (one on the Staff) and 19 other ranks. Medals to the 3rd Dragoon Guards are also scarce. Those to the 33rd Regiment are popular as they led the attack on Magdala and were awarded two Victoria Crosses.

Obverse

Reverse

Ashantee War Medal
1873—1874

This medal was authorised in June 1874 and was awarded to the Army and Royal Navy, together with local units. Only one bar was issued this being for Coomassie. It was also issued without a bar.

The naming is in engraved upright serif capitals and, on the Army medals, usually included the dates, 1873–74, at the end. Those to the Royal Navy are dated 73–74. The medal awarded to Major General Sir G. P. Colley is not dated. This was obviously due to insufficient space on the rim after engraving all other details. Sir George Colley's Ashantee Medal with Coomassie bar, together with his China 1857–60, with two bars, were sold by Sotheby's in February 1970, for £280.00.

As with many other medals, the Ashantee issue provides several instances of "rare to regiment", including Colley's, as he was with the 2nd Foot. Other examples are those to Lieut. F. Clowes, 30th Foot and Major J. Lazenby, 100th Foot.

Reverse

East and West Africa Medal
1887—1900

This medal is of exactly the same design as the Ashantee 1873–1874, but slightly thinner. Except for Mwele 1895 it was never issued without a bar and, for this expedition, the award "Mwele" was impressed on the rim, to the left of the claw with the date "1895" or "1895–6" to the right. Apart from being thinner, there is one other difference in that on the Ashantee issues the dates "1873–74" or "73–74" are engraved on the rim.

Twenty one bars were awarded but, unfortunately, it is not possible to list them in this book. In addition, two others, 1896–97 and 1896–99, are also quoted in some reference books. Liwondi 1893, Juba River 1893, Lake Nyassa 1893 and Dawkita 1897 are the rarest and, although more are said to have been awarded for Dawkita 1897 than Lake Nyassa 1893, the first mentioned is rarer on the market.

There are several styles of naming.

Afghanistan Medal

1878—1880

The six bars listed below were granted with this medal which was authorised in March 1881.

Ali Musjid, Peiwar Kotal, Charasia, Kabul, Ahmed Khel, Kandahar.

The maximum number of bars on any one medal is four, and these are usually to the 5th Goorkhas or the 72nd Regt.

Probably the best known event was the march from Kabul to Kandahar under General (later Lord) Roberts but, once again, it is a disaster which seems to have the greatest appeal to the majority of collectors. This occurred on 22nd July 1880 when General Burrow's force was badly defeated at Maiwand. The 66th Regiment suffered severe casualties in this action and medals to those killed are eagerly sought after, and the last auction price for one of these was £50.00.

The medal was issued, without bars, to those who did not take part in the battles.

Reverse

Kabul to Kandahar Star

1880

As the name of this star suggests, it was awarded to all who had taken part in the famous march, of just over 300 miles, between the 9th and 31st August, which the force under General Roberts achieved when going to the relief of the besieged city of Kandahar.

The main British regiments to receive this star were the 9th Lancers, 2/60th, 72nd and 92nd, with a detachment of the 66th. It is rare to the 59th and 65th regiments.

Made by H. Jenkins & Sons, Birmingham, these stars were struck in bronze and, to British recipients, are named on the reverse in impressed plain capital letters. Those issued to Indian troops have similar naming, but engraved.

All who qualified for this star would have received the Afghanistan medal with Kandahar bar, but not necessarily for Kabul. For example the 60th Regiment got bars for Ahmed Khel and Kandahar.

Obverse

Reverse

Cape of Good Hope General Service Medal

1880—1897

Issued in accordance with Army Order 841 of 1900, and the following three bars were authorised:

Transkei, Basutoland, Bechuanaland.

It was never awarded without a bar.

Overall this is a scarce issue, and medals with all three bars are of the highest rarity, as only thirteen were awarded. A medal with confirmed bars for Transkei and Bechuanaland would also be rare as it would cover service between Sept 1880 and July 1897.

The naming is usually engraved in upright serif capitals but some medals are impressed in rather large capital letters, and it has been noticed that it is usually necessary to reverse the medal when reading this type of naming.

British regiments did not take part in any of the three campaigns, but some individuals received the medal, mainly officers, and the parent unit is usually included in the naming.

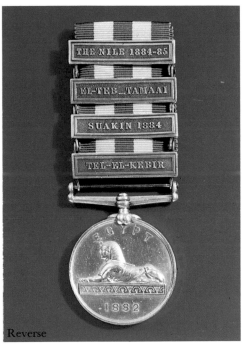

Reverse

Egypt Medal

1882—1889

The undermentioned 13 bars were awarded with this medal which has two types of reverses, the first bearing the date 1882 and the other being undated.

Alexandria 11th July, Tel-El-Kebir, El-Teb, Tamaai, El-Teb-Tamaai, Suakin 1884, The Nile 1884–85, Abu Klea, Kirbekan, Suakin 1885, Tofrek, Gemaizah 1888, Toski 1889.

The first two bars were for the 1882 campaign but those for later actions also appear on the dated medal. As medals without bars were awarded, for both periods, it would be possible for a recipient to receive the dated medal and then later bars. Toski 1889 is the rarest bar to British troops.

A number of ships from the Royal Navy took part in these campaigns and personnel received either the dated or undated medal, together with any appropriate bars.

Naming is usually engraved in sloping serif capital letters.

North West Canada Medal
1885

In September 1885 this medal was issued to all who had taken part in the suppression of the rebellion led by Louis Riel, who had previously been the cause of trouble which resulted in the Red River expedition of 1870. One bar, for Saskatchewan, was granted with this issue, and many recipients received it without a bar.

Unlike the earlier Fenian disturbances of 1866 and 1870, British troops were not engaged although a few British officers were present. Numerous Canadian units took part and, of these, medals to the North West Mounted Police are possibly the most sought after. The crew of the steamer Northcote were awarded the medal and this is a rare issue.

These medals were issued unnamed but many were named subsequently. Therefore, it is not possible to describe a standard pattern of naming, but those seen to the N.W.M.P. have usually had impressed serifed capital letters.

Reverse

Ashanti Star

1896

This gun metal star was awarded to those who had taken part in the expedition against King Prempeh, between 7th December 1895 and 17th January 1896.

The 2nd battalion of the West Yorkshire Regiment was the only British battalion present in any strength, although detachments were present from several others, as well as elements from supporting arms.

This star was issued unnamed but, in the case of the West Yorkshire Regiment, they were named at the expense of the Colonel.

Coomassie figures prominently in British war medals for it was again captured in this campaign, as in 1873-74, and this was to happen for a third time in 1900.

Being unnamed, this star is of far greater interest if part of a group of named medals, as it is then possible to check on the recipient and, excluding the West Yorkshire regiment, it is certain to be quite rare.

Obverse

Reverse

British South Africa Company's Medals

There are four of these medals, each with a different reverse, as detailed below.

1) Matabeleland 1893
2) Rhodesia 1896
3) Mashonaland 1897
4) Without place or date, but with bar Mashonaland 1890.

Four bars were also authorised, as follows: Mashonaland 1890, Matabeleland 1893, Rhodesia 1896, Mashonaland 1897.

The Mashonaland 1890 is the rarest and this was not authorised until 1926. Those who had already received medals for any of the other campaigns were asked to surrender them when claiming this medal. They were then issued the Mashonaland 1890 with any appropriate bars. There were four entitled to the Mashonaland 1890 medal with three bars, but it appears that only one was issued.

Naming is usually by rather heavily engraved plain capitals.

Central Africa Medal

1891—1898

There were two issues of this medal, the first being in 1895 and the second in 1899. The 1895 issue has a small swivelling ring for suspension and is without bar, whilst the later type carries a plain straight swivelling suspender, with the bar "Central Africa 1894–98". The first type is scarce and the second quite rare and, as they are the same design as the East and West Africa, 1887–1900, the new collector should be careful to distinguish between these medals. British troops were not employed on the operations for which these medals were awarded but there is at least one, with bar, known to have been gained by a British officer and named to his parent regiment. This was Major F. Trollope, Grenadier Guards.

A few British Naval officers and native seamen, all of whom appear to have received the medal and bar, are listed in a copy of a medal roll which is headed "Naval Corps".

Reverse

India General Service Medal

1895–1902

Instituted in 1896, after twenty three bars had been authorised for the India General Service, 1854–1895, this medal, with minor variation, was also awarded by Edward VII.

The following seven bars were issued:– Defence of Chitral 1895, Relief of Chitral 1895, Punjab Frontier 1897–98, Malakand 1897, Samana 1897, Tirah 1897–98, Waziristan 1901–02.

The first is by far the rarest as it was only awarded to the small garrison, under Brevet-Major C. V. F. Townshend, which consisted of less than 600 Indian troops. It is especially rare in bronze. Malakand is not too common, as it was again mainly issued to Indian troops. Some books are misleading in this respect as, although British regiments formed part of the Malakand Field-Force, they did not receive this bar. It is possible that a few men from British regiments received the Malakand bar but, most probably, because they were attached to the Indian Army. A medal with Malakand bar, named to a British regiment, would be rare.

Bronze medals were also awarded with any of the bars listed. It is not possible to get a single bar for either Samana 1897 or Tirah 1897–98.

Most medals are engraved in running script but those to the D.C.L.I. are very crudely engraved and the 2nd H.L.I. are usually found engraved in upright sans serif capitals. Some Indian Army units have impressed serif capitals.

The Edward VII medal, with Waziristan 1901–02 bar, is thinner than the Victorian ones, and the date 1895 was removed from the reverse. This bar would be rare to British troops and is quite scarce in bronze.

As the Relief of Chitral bar was issued without lugs it is quite common to see this bar fitted out of correct sequence, at the top. Also, it can be found with holes drilled at the sides and then other bars fixed to it by metal loops.

The more sought after medals are those to the Dorset Regiment and the Gordon Highlanders, as they were distinguished in the attack on the Dargai Heights, 20th October 1897. Pte.

Reverse

S. Vickery, Dorset Regiment and Piper Geo. Findlater, Gordon Highlanders were both awarded the Victoria Cross for their gallantry in this action. A medal to the 36th Sikhs, which includes the Samana 1897 bar, is also desirable. One Indian officer and twenty men from this regiment, all of whom were killed, most gallantly defended Fort Gulistan, which barred the approach to the Afridi Hills. In recognition of their splendid defence a memorial to them was erected at Amritsar. The Malakand bar is also popular as, in addition to being the second scarcest on the Queen's medal, it can be associated with Sir Winston Churchill who, of course, served in that campaign and wrote "The Story of the Malakand Field Force".

At the present time the India 1897 medals sell in the lower price range and, with the exception of the Defence of Chitral bar, can be found on dealers' lists from below £10.00 up to about £15.00. This includes the quite scarce bronze issue with Malakand 1897 bar. The last recorded auction price (September 1972) for a silver Defence of Chitral was £80.

Reverse

Queen's Sudan
1896–1898

The Queen's Sudan medal was instituted in 1899 for all personnel of the British, Egyptian and Indian Armies who helped in the re-conquest of the Sudan.

No bars were authorised for this medal, which was issued in silver and bronze.

Naming is usually in engraved sloping serif capitals but there are other styles, as some medals are impressed in plain capitals and those to the Sudanese troops bear Arabic inscriptions.

The most sought after medals are those to the 21st Lancers for their famous charge at Omdurman, in which Winston Churchill participated when attached from the 4th Hussars. Despite the fact that this charge, like that at Balaklava, was really an example of military ineptitude, medals to participants still appeal to most collectors and realise much higher prices than those to other regiments.

A rare medal to the Royal Navy and Royal Marines, the roll lists only 44 recipients.

Reverse

East and Central Africa
1897—1898

Approval for the award of this medal was given in Army Order 29 of 29th February 1899 and the following four bars were granted:– Lubwa's, Uganda 1897–98, 1898, and Uganda 1899.

The bar for Lubwa's is usually found in conjunction with that for Uganda 1897–98, but single bar medals are recorded. It was never issued without a bar.

Bronze medals are known, but they are extremely scarce on the market.

British regiments did not take part in any of the expeditions, but medals are known to Sergt. S. W. Bone, S. Lancs. Regt. and Sergt. R. Thompson, Seaforth Highlanders. These provide examples of 'rare to regiment' and, no doubt, there were other individuals similarly detached from their parent units. Some British officers and a number of civilians also qualified.

Naming is usually in engraved seriffed capitals but the impressed style is also seen on some medals.

Royal Niger Company's Medals

1886—1897

These medals were issued by the Royal Niger Company for services in several punitive expeditions in the Company's territory between 1886 and 1897. They were designed and made by Spink and Son Limited, London, in silver and bronze. The bronze medals have a bar reading "Nigeria" only. Neither of them was issued without a bar.

In silver they are extremely rare, being awarded only to white officers of the Company, officers and non-commissioned officers of H.M's Forces and Royal Niger Company Constabulary. "British Battles and Medals"— L. L. Gordon (4th edition—revised E. C. Joslin) gives a total of 97 being issued. The naming on these medals is usually in rather bold, upright, impressed serifed capitals.

The bronze issues are impressed with a number only, which is presumably that of the recipient.

Reverse

Ashanti Medal

1900

This was the first campaign medal to be issued bearing the head of King Edward VII and only one bar was authorised, namely Kumassi. This bar is somewhat unusual in that it was awarded both to the garrison who defended Kumassi and to those who formed the two columns which took part in its relief. On other occasions, Lucknow, Chitral, Mafeking etc., "Defence" and "Relief" bars were sanctioned. Medals without bars were also issued.

British regiments did not take part in this campaign probably because, with the Boer War still in progress, they could not be spared, but some officers and N.C.O's were present. Medals to them, named to their parent regiments, would be rare.

Naming is usually in impressed upright plain capitals but medals to officers were often engraved with serifed letters.

Reverse

Reverse

China Medal

1900

The award of this medal was confirmed by King Edward VII in January 1902, and the following three bars were authorised:
Taku Forts, Defence of Legations and Relief of Pekin.

The 2nd Royal Welch Fusiliers received the Relief of Pekin bar, being the only British Infantry regiment present in strength, and it would be rare to any other. Defence of Legations is the rarest bar and this was gained mainly by the Royal Marine Light Infantry, but some civilians also received it. One of the three Royal Navy recipients of this bar is Chief Bosun H. Swannell, who was awarded the Conspicuous Gallantry Medal during the defence. His medals were sold by Sotheby's in January 1972 and the price recorded for them was £1,100.00. At the same sale a pair of family medals including China 1900 with Defence of Legations bar, made £260.00.

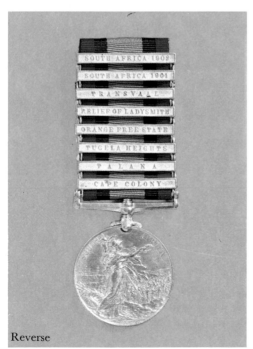

Reverse

Queen's South Africa Medal

1899—1902

As twenty six bars were awarded with this medal it is not possible to list them. There are two different reverse strikings, with the first having the wreath held by Britannia pointing to the letter "R" in Africa whilst, on the second, it points to the "F". Medals without bars were also issued in bronze.

Naming is mostly in plain impressed capitals.

The majority of medals awarded to Lord Strathcona's Horse have the dates 1899–1900, in relief, on the reverse. These are rare and sell for £200.00. The Defence of Mafeking bar is greatly sought after and, in 1972, a London dealer listed one at £105.00.

Numerous collectors now like to have medals to those killed or wounded. The publication of "Casualties of the South African Field Force" (Oaklands Book Division) made the Q.S.A. particularly suitable for this type of collecting.

King's South Africa Medal

1901—1902

After the death of Queen Victoria, and the war still being in progress, King Edward VII authorised this medal to all who were serving in South Africa on or after 1st January 1902 and who would complete eighteen months service before 1st June 1902. It is a very rare medal to the Royal Navy.

Only two bars were issued, these being South Africa 1901 and South Africa 1902. Presumably the eighteen months had to be continuous service as many received these two date bars on their Queen's medal, not qualifying for the K.S.A.

The King's medal was only issued in silver but it is possible to get it without a bar, as nearly 600 nurses received the medal only.

Although K.S.A. medals with single bars have been known for a long time; such issues have only recently been authenticated.

Reverse

Transport Medal

1899—1902

Sanctioned in November 1903, this medal was awarded to Masters, 1st, 2nd and 3rd Officers, 1st, 2nd and 3rd Engineers, Pursers and Surgeons of merchant vessels employed in the transport of troops to the Boer War and the Boxer rebellion in China, 1900. Two bars were authorised, these being—S. Africa 1899–1902 and China 1900.

The Transport Medal can be classified as a scarce issue, as less than two thousand were awarded, and with two bars it is quite rare. The China 1900 is much the scarcer of the two bars.

Naming is in impressed serifed capital letters and only the initials and surname are normally given except for medals to Masters, where the words "In Command" follow after the name.

Copies of the official medal roll are available giving shipping line and ship, and it is therefore possible to establish on which ship a recipient served.

Reverse

Reverse

Africa General Service Medal

1902

The issue of this medal was sanctioned in 1902 and the forty five bars listed below have been issued. These are grouped in alphabetical/geographical and then alphabetical order and not by dates.

East Africa 1902, East Africa 1904, East Africa 1905, East Africa 1906, East Africa 1913, East Africa 1913/14, East Africa 1914, East Africa 1915, East Africa 1918, Jubaland 1900–01, Jubaland 1917/18, N. Nigeria (1900–01), N. Nigeria 1902, N. Nigeria 1903, N. Nigeria 1903–04, N. Nigeria 1904, N. Nigeria 1906, Somaliland 1901, Somaliland 1902–04, Somaliland 1908–10, Somaliland 1920, S. Nigeria (1901), S. Nigeria 1902, S. Nigeria 1902–03, S. Nigeria 1903, S. Nigeria 1903–04, S. Nigeria 1904, S. Nigeria 1904–05, S. Nigeria 1905, S. Nigeria 1905–06, W. Africa 1906, W. Africa 1908, W. Africa 1909–10, Aro 1901–02, B.C.A. 1899–1900, Gambia (1901),

Jidballi (1904), Kenya (1952–56), Kissi 1905, Lango 1901, Nandi 1905–06, Nigeria 1918, Nyasaland 1915, Shimber Berris 1914–15, Uganda 1900. Where dates are in brackets they do not appear on the medal.

There are two obverse strikings of the Edward VII issue, one having the head of the King in much higher relief; and the qualifying dates for the Kenya bar covers the period when a change in legend took place from "Elizabeth II D.G. Br. Omn. Regina F:D" to "Elizabeth II Dei Gratia Regina F.D.". Edward VII medals were also awarded in bronze but apart from the Somaliland 1902–04 bar, which is very scarce, all other bars are rare. On silver medals the more common bars are Somaliland 1902–04, and Somaliland 1908–10 and this applies mainly to the first mentioned when issued to the Royal Navy or African regiments, as it is scarce, often rare, to British regiments. A verified medal to the Royal Navy, with these two bars, would also be rare. The Jidballi bar is always found in conjunction with Somaliland 1902–04, and this combination is again either scarce or rare, depending on regiment, to British recipients.

All King George V issues are very scarce, and no British regiments received any of the bars, although individuals, mainly officers, did qualify for many of them. A few ships from the Royal Navy took part in the Somaliland 1920 campaign, as did a small number of R.A.F. personnel. Among these ships was the Ark Royal, which was a seaplane carrier, and not the aircraft carrier which earned so much fame during the 1939–45 war.

An African General Service medal worth a special note is the one awarded to Lieut. E. S. Carey, R.N., who received the bars Somaliland 1902–04, Jidballi, as the latter bar is unique to the Royal Navy. This medal, together with his Queen's South Africa, no bars, was sold in Glendining's sale of September 1972, where a price of £240.00 was recorded.

There are various types of naming, as is to be expected for a medal covering such a long period but, as a general rule, medals to the Army are impressed in small plain capitals, those to the Royal Navy have larger impressed serifed capitals whilst the R.A.F. naming is in taller plain capitals, except for medals with Kenya bar, where those seen were engraved.

Natal Rebellion Medal

1906

The Goldsmiths and Silversmiths Company, London (now Garrard & Co. Ltd.) designed and manufactured this medal, which was authorised in May 1907. One bar was issued which was "1906". It was also awarded without a bar and, in fact, although not so sought after, these medals are scarcer.

British troops did not take any part in this campaign, but full details of units who received the medal are given in "British Battles and Medals" by Major L. L. Gordon (4th edition—revised by E. C. Joslin), which is the most comprehensive reference book available on British campaign medals.

Among these units are the Indian Stretcher Bearers in which the well known Indian politician, the late M. K. Ghandi, served as a Sergeant Major.

Naming is usually in rather tall plain impressed capitals, but all the medals seen to officers have been in engraved running script.

Reverse

Tibet Medal

1903—1904

In February 1905, King Edward VII gave approval for the award of this medal to all who had taken part in the Tibet Mission and to the troops accompanying it. Only one bar was authorised, this being for Gyantse, but it was also awarded without bar. Bronze medals with bars and without were also issued to followers.

The force was mainly from the Indian Army, and the only British Regiment in any strength was the 1st Battalion Royal Fusiliers. Other British troops included Mountain Batteries of the Royal Artillery and machine gun sections from the Norfolk Regiment and Royal Irish Rifles. One authority also lists the Royal Irish Regiment but this could be an error, as Tibet is not mentioned in the regimental history. Eight men of the King's Own Regiment received this medal and a number were awarded to civilians.

Naming is mostly engraved in running script.

Reverse

Obverse

India General Service Medal

1908–1935

In common with previous India General Service medals this one was issued in silver and bronze. It was the last campaign medal to be awarded during the reign of King Edward VII, but only one bar was issued on the medal bearing his effigy. This was "North West Frontier 1908" and it was struck in both silver and bronze. The latter is very much scarcer.

Twelve bars were issued during the period covered and these are as follows:–

North West Frontier 1908 (Feb–May 1908), Abor 1911–12 (Oct 1911–Apr 1912), Afghanistan N.W.F. 1919 (May–Aug 1919), Mahsud 1919–20 (Nov 1919–May 1920), Waziristan 1919–21 (May 1919–Jan 1921), Malabar 1921–22 (Aug 1921–Feb 1922), Waziristan 1921–24 (Dec 1921–Mar 1924), Waziristan 1925 (March–May 1925), North West Frontier 1930–31 (Apr 1930–Mar 1931), Burma 1930–32 (Dec 1930–Mar 1932), Mohmand 1933

(Jul–Oct 1933), North West Frontier 1935 (Jan–Nov 1935).

The rarest bar is Waziristan 1925 which, as far as is known, was only awarded to the RAF. As a point of interest, the rarest bar gained by the RAF is Burma 1930–32. This is extremely rare to them, as only 14 are shown on the roll. Strangely enough, although this is based on experience only, as actual details are not available, the Burma bar 1930–32 bar appears to be rare to a British recipient in the Royal Artillery.

There are two types of the King George V medal as the first issue has the legend "Georgivs V Kaisar-I-Hind," which started with the Abor 1911–12 bar, and the second is "Georgivs 'V·D·G· Britt·Omn·Rex·Et·Indiae·Imp'" This change took place with the North West Frontier 1930–31 bar.

There are several styles of naming; the Edward VII medals are engraved in running script, and the same applies to Abor 1911–12 although, in this case, the engraving is much larger. The most common naming is the impressed type, small capital letters, without serifs, but the pre 1930 medals to the RAF have a distinctive style of impressed naming, with the plain capitals being much taller.

Abor 1911–12 is the next rarest bar, and in bronze could be classified as very rare. Mahsud 1919–20 and Mohmand 1933 are scarce to Europeans and, although the first mentioned turns up as a single bar, any such medal must be considered doubtful, as a recipient is almost certain to have qualified for Waziristan 1919–21. Malabar 1921–22 is also scarce to British regiments as only three infantry battalions were engaged. A squadron of the 2nd Dragoon Guards (Queen's Bays) were also present.

Although medals with two or more bars to Indian Army units are often seen they are not common to British infantry regiments, and the most usual combination is likely to be the bars for Waziristan 1919–21 and Waziristan 1921–24. Four and five bar medals to Indian regiments are seen listed but they would be extremely difficult to verify. It would be possible to establish that the regiment qualified for the particular bars but almost impossible to confirm that the recipient was entitled, unless awarded to an officer. With the post 1930 issue, apart from R.A., R.E., R. Sigs. etc. it would be extremely unusual to find a medal with two or more bars to a British regiment.

Naval General Service Medal

1915–1964

As with all General Service Medals this one was never awarded without a bar. Fifteen bars were issued altogether and these are detailed below.

Persian Gulf 1909–1914, Iraq 1919–20, N. W. Persia 1920, Palestine 1936–39, S. E. Asia 1945–46, Minesweeping 1945–51, Palestine 1945–48, Yangtze 1949, Bomb and Mine Clearance 1945–53, Malaya, Bomb and Mine Clearance Mediterranean, Cyprus, Near East, Arabian Peninsulan, Brunei.

The rarest bar is N.W. Persia 1920 as there were only eight recipients. Next in rarity is Iraq 1919–20 (128 issued), although it must be mentioned that figures are not available for later bars such as Bomb & Mine Clearance, Mediterranean.

One of the most sought after bars is Yangtze 1949, especially if the recipient can be established as serving on HMS Amethyst. This is probably due to the fact that the "Yangtze Incident" is still fresh in the memory of many people and, with the present tendency for many collectors to concentrate on the Victorian era, provides one of the few instances where more recent campaign medals are considered to be as desirable as those of an earlier period.

Based again only on experience, the bar for Cyprus, to the Royal Navy, does not seem at all common on the market. When this bar appears on a list it is usually to the Royal Marines. The two "Bomb and Mine Clearance" bars are also rarely seen.

Naming in the "Persian Gulf" issues is by large impressed serif type capitals and includes the name of the ship. The "Iraq 1919–20" has smaller and plain impressed capitals and, also, this medal has a fixed suspender. Since the "Palestine 1936–39" issue naming seems to have remained constant, again being small plain impressed capitals and with just R.N. or R.M., not ship's name.

Although one of the more common bars, that for Persian Gulf 1909–15, does provide an instance of rarity as, like the first Naval General Service, 1793–1840, a few military personnel received it. This bar was awarded to thirteen

Obverse

Army officers and, also, to one member of the Indian Police.

If one counts the Geo. V fixed suspender as a different type there are six varieties of this medal. They are:–

1) Geo. V with the legend "Georgivs V Britt: Omd: Rex et Ind: Imp" and swivel suspender.
2) Fixed suspender with same legend.
3) Geo VI with the legend "Georgivs VI G: Br: Omn: Rex et Indiae Imp:"
4) Geo VI with the legend "Georgivs VI Dei: Gra: Britt: Omn: Rex: Fid. Def+."
5) Elizabeth II with the legend "Elizabeth II D: G: Br: Omn: Regina F:D:"
6) Elizabeth II with the legend "Elizabeth II Dei. Gratia. Regina F.D.+".

This medal also provides the somewhat unusual instance where the same bar applies to different issues, as Malaya appears on both King George VI and Queen Elizabeth II.

Obverse

1914 Star

(5th August—22nd November 1914)

If you collect war medals for what they really represent—courage, endurance, hardship, suffering and sacrifice, then one might truly say that this bronze star is the first of the foremost, commemorating, as it does, the earliest period of the greatest war of all time.

Generally referred to as the Mons Star, it was authorised in April 1917 to those who had served in France or Belgium between the qualifying dates mentioned above. In October 1919 King George V sanctioned a bar "5th Aug–22nd Nov. 1914", and this is sewn on to the ribbon. It was only awarded to those who actually served, under fire, during or between the dates indicated.

This star is scarce to the Royal Navy, as only those who served on land for the requisite period could qualify. It is rare to Canadians and a few Australians are said to have qualified.

Obverse

1914-1915 Star

The remarks applied to the 1914 Star would, naturally enough, be equally appropriate to this one, as the period it covers includes major battles such as Festubert, Hooge, Loos.

The star was authorised in 1918 and is different to the 1914 Star in that the date on the centre scroll has been changed to 1914–15 and the months "Aug" and "Nov" on the smaller scrolls have been omitted. Awarded to all personnel who served at sea or on the establishment of a unit in a theatre of war during the qualifying period. The silver rosette worn on the ribbon of the 1914 Star to denote the award of the bar is not worn on the ribbon of the 1914–15 Star.

British War Medal

1914—1920

Originally authorised in 1919 for services in the Great War, this award was later extended to 1919–20 to cover operations in Russia, the Eastern Baltic and other areas, and also for post-war mine-clearance at sea.

It commemorates the most terrible battles in which British forces have ever fought, such as those on the Somme and at Ypres, to mention just two, as well as the tremendous Naval engagement in the Battle of Jutland.

The significance of this medal is illustrated by the undermentioned extract in respect of Lieut. M. R. H. Morley, K.O.Y.L.I.

"On July 1st 1916 his bn. was engaged near Thiepval in the first assault of the Battle of the Somme. He was twice wounded while leading the remnants of four companies from the first to the third line of enemy trenches, but refused to go back and remained at the head of his men till he fell for the last time."

Reverse

Mercantile Marine War Medal

This bronze medal was issued by the Board of Trade to all who had served at sea on at least one voyage through a danger zone.

Unlike the Transport Medal issued for South Africa 1899–1902 and China 1900, this medal was awarded to both officers and men; and some women also qualified. It was never awarded singly, as all recipients were entitled to the British War medal, with many also receiving the Victory medal.

Groups consisting of 1914–15 Star, British War Medal, Mercantile Marine War Medal and Victory Medal are also possible. This combination of medals, with 1914 Star instead of 1914–15 Star, would be unusual, as a recipient would have had to transfer from one of the other services to the Mercantile Marine.

Naming is in impressed plain capitals and usually included the Christian name. When awarded to Australians the name of the country is often included.

Reverse

Allied Victory Medal

1914—1920

Obverse

This bronze medal was awarded to all personnel who served in any theatre of operations, or at sea, during the Great War. Unlike the British War Medal, 1914–20, it was never awarded alone. The first medals were in dull bronze but later issues, and these are the majority, were gilded.

The allied countries issued Victory medals of the same basic design as the British and the rainbow ribbon was used for all of them.

The bronze oak leaf, for being mentioned in despatches in the Great War, is worn on this ribbon. The exceptions would be to those who only qualified for the British War Medal, when the "mention" could then be worn on that ribbon.

The most usual naming is as described for the British War Medal, and again there are several styles. When awarded to Army officers both these medals have just rank, initials and surname as the regiment is not given.

Territorial Force War Medal

1914—1919

Reverse

Issued in bronze, this medal was awarded to all members of the Territorial Force, including Nursing Sisters, who volunteered for overseas service on or before 30th September, 1914 and who rendered such service during the Great War. Precise details of qualification can be found in "Ribbons and Medals" by Dorling and Guille.

The dates 1914–1919 on the reverse are not consistent with the qualifying period, as eligibility terminated on 11th November 1918. The main reason for the introduction of this medal was to reward personnel who had volunteered for overseas service but were ineligible for the 1914 Star or 1914–15 Star. Groups of medals which include the Territorial Force War Medal and one or the other of these stars are said to exist, but this is not possible according to the regulations. It is worn immediately after the Victory Medal.

General Service Medal (Army & R.A.F.)

1918–1964

Instituted in January 1923, this medal has the undermentioned bars.

S. Persia (Nov 1918–Jan 1919), Kurdistan (May–Dec 1919 and Mar–Jun 1923), Iraq (Dec 1919–Nov 1920), N.W. Persia (Aug–Dec 1920), Southern Desert–Iraq (Jan–Jun 1928), Northern Kurdistan (Mar–Jun 1932), Palestine (Apr 1936–Sept 1939), S.E. Asia 1945–46, Bomb & Mine Clearance 1945–49, Bomb & Mine Clearance 1945–56, Palestine 1945–48 (Sept. 1945–Jan 1948), Malaya (Jan 1948–Jul 1960), Cyprus (Apr 1955–Apr 1959), Near East (Oct–Dec 1956), Arabian Peninsula (Jan 1957–June 1960), Brunei (8–23 Jan 1962).

As is to be expected with a medal that covers such a long span of years, there are several different issues and types, and these are detailed below:–

1) Coinage head Geo.V and legend "Georgivs V.D.G.Britt. Omn:Rex et Ind: Imp."
2) Crowned head Geo.V and legend "Georgivs V.D.G.Britt. Omn. Rex. Et. Indiae.Imp."
3) Crowned head Geo.VI and legend "Georgivs VI D: G: Br: Omn: Rex Et Indiae Imp:".
4) Crowned head Geo.VI and legend "Georgivs VI Dei Gra: Britt: Omn: Rex Fid: Def+"
5) Crowned head Elizabeth II and legend "Elizabeth II D.G.: Br:Omn:Regina F.D.+".
6) Crowned head Elizabeth II and legend "Elizabeth II Dei Gratia Regina F.D.+".

With the Geo VI and Elizabeth II issues there are also variations such as swivel and fixed suspenders.

The rarest bars are Southern Desert – Iraq, Northern Kurdistan, Bomb and Mine Clearance 1945–56. The Northern Kurdistan bar is the only one on the Geo V crowned head issue and this is a very rare medal on the market.

Reverse

Although all authorities quote the bar "Bomb & Mine Clearance 1945–56" at least one medal is known to have the bar "Bomb & Mine Clearance 1945–53", and it appears to be genuine (see illustration).

There are various styles of naming. Medals to the Army have the small impressed capitals whilst those to the RAF on Geo.V issues have the taller impressed lettering with plain capitals. George VI and Elizabeth II medals to the RAF have the naming engraved, although some with the Palestine bar are found in the impressed lettering and the engraved ones for this period are in a different style from that found on later issues.

It is not unusual to find a medal with two or more bars that have been fixed by pins (similar to that in the suspender) which extend from outer rivet hole to outer rivet hole. This method was adopted by the Army in order to make it easier for a receipient to fit any further bars he received. As this practice was only adopted in recent years it might not be generally known, and a new collector could reject a medal because it was different from others he had seen when in fact it was genuine.

Reverse

India General Service Medal

1936—1939

Instituted in August 1938, this medal, which had the two undermentioned bars authorised, replaced the India General Service 1908. It was never issued without bar.

North West Frontier, 1936–37, North West Frontier, 1937–39.

There are two types, as one was made at the Royal Mint and another by the Calcutta Mint. The most noticeable variation is on the suspenders, as the British issue has a flange and pin fitment whilst the one made in Calcutta has the claw fitting. Another difference is that the initials of the designer are below the King's head on the Royal Mint striking, but they do not appear on the Calcutta issue.

Naming is usually in small impressed plain capitals but some medals to the R.A.F. are engraved.

Medals with both bars, to British regiments, are very scarce on the market.

Obverse

1939-1945 Star

Awarded for service covering the period of the Second World War, this unnamed star represents epics such as Dunkirk, Narvik and the Battle of Britain. Aircrew who fought in the latter received a bar, which is the only one awarded with this star. When wearing medal ribbons only, the Battle of Britain bar is denoted by a gilt rosette sewn on to the appropriate ribbon.

For the Navy and Army the general qualification was six months in an operational area, but there are exceptions to this, and full details can be found in several of the reference books mentioned in the bibliography. The same period applied for the Merchant Navy, with the proviso that at least one voyage was made through an operational area. In the R.A.F. aircrew with two months service in an operational area, which included operations against the enemy, qualified. Non-aircrew had to complete six months service in an operational army command.

Atlantic Star

Like all others issued in the Second World War this star was unnamed and, as the name indicates, was awarded to commemorate the Battle of the Atlantic, the qualifying period being from 3rd September 1939 to 8th May 1945.

The basic requirement was six months service at sea but there are differences in qualifications for the Royal Navy and Merchant Navy. Full details are again readily available in other easily obtainable reference books. Some recipients qualified for either Air Crew Europe or France and Germany bars, but it is not possible to have both. When wearing only ribbons a silver rosette is worn to signify the award of a bar.

Coastal Command of the R.A.F. and certain Army personnel, could qualify for this star.

An outstanding example of an Army award is the D.C.M. group to Sergeant W. A. Challington, Cameron Highlanders. This included an Atlantic Star and sold at Sotheby's in January 1971 for £210.00.

Obverse

The Air Crew Europe Star

Of the eight stars issued for service in the Second World War this is the only one that has remained quite scarce on the market and, when one takes into account the vast efforts of R.A.F. Bomber Command, it is difficult to know the reason for this. One possibility is that many who were entitled just did not bother to submit claims which, in view of the generally poor quality of all the stars, as well as being unnamed, is readily understandable.

Either Atlantic or France and Germany bars could also be gained with this star, which are again denoted by a silver rose emblem when wearing only ribbons.

Being the only Second World War Star which sells for more than two pounds, copies have been made, mostly for the purpose of replacing originals that have been lost, but these could be deceptive to an inexperienced collector.

Obverse

Obverse

Africa Star

As this star symbolises events in British military history such as Wavell's brilliant campaign during the early period of the desert war, together with Montgomery's final defeat of Rommel in North Africa, it provides an outstanding example of why medal collectors deplore the decision to issue Second World War stars unnamed, thereby making it impossible to associate them directly with any of the well known battles.

The qualifying period was from 10th June 1940 to 12th May 1943, and service of one day or more in an operational area gained entitlement. It was also awarded for service in Abyssinia, Eritrea, Malta and Somaliland.

Those with the requisite qualifications could gain one of the following bars:– 8th Army, 1st Army, North Africa 1942–43.

When wearing just the ribbons entitlement to these bars is signified by a silver arabic numeral "8" or "1" and a silver rosette for last mentioned.

Obverse

The Pacific Star

Awarded for service in the Pacific theatre of operations between 8th December, 1941 and 2nd September, 1945, both dates inclusive, this star appears to have been gained more by the Royal Navy than the other services.

Recipients who later would have qualified for the Burma Star received, instead, a bar, "Burma" which was sewn on to the ribbon of the Pacific Star.

When wearing ribbons only, entitlement to this bar is indicated by a silver rosette. It is possible to gain this award without qualifying for the 1939–1945 Star, as this applied to those who served in the Pacific zone after 2nd March 1945 up to 2nd September 1945. In such cases a time qualification of six months did not apply.

Australian forces played an important part in the Pacific operations and the majority of the stars issued to them are named. This applies to all other stars and medals awarded to Australians for service in the 1939–1945 War.

The Burma Star

The qualifying dates for the award of this star are between 11th December 1941 and 2nd September 1945, both dates inclusive. As with the Pacific Star, the same special rule applied for service after 2nd March 1945, whereby previous entitlement to the 1939/45 Star was not necessary. A bar "Pacific" was authorised for those who would have been entitled to the Pacific Star had they not previously qualified for the Burma Star.

A silver rosette again indicates entitlement to the bar when wearing only ribbons.

Being unnamed, it is usually impossible to associate a star with an individual, or even any specific battle. Therefore, the only way, to represent the great achievements of the 14th Army and its famous units, such as the Chindits, apart from a named gallantry medal, is by the inclusion of a Burma Star in a collection of medals.

Obverse

The Italy Star

In addition to service in Italy and Sicily, for which the qualifying dates were from 11th June 1943 to 8th May 1945, this star could also be gained by serving in the Aegean, the Dodecanese, Corsica, Greece, Sardinia, Yugoslavia and Elba. As with several of the other Second World War stars it could also be awarded without first qualifying for the 1939/45 Star, and entry into Austria during the closing stages of the war also counted. Visits of even thirty days duration provided they were authorised by a Commander-in-Chief, also gained entitlement. These rather easy qualifications must have seemed unfair to those who had taken part in the invasion of Sicily, the first landings on Italian soil, and such bitter actions as Anzio and Cassino.

Once again, the medal collector can only represent such battles, and this whole hard fought campaign, by the inclusion of another unnamed star which, to say the least, is not even particularly well made.

Obverse

Obverse

The France and Germany Star

This star was awarded for service in France, Belgium, Holland and Germany, the qualifying period being from D Day (6th June 1944) to V.E. Day (8th May 1945).

Personnel who had previously gained entitlement to either the Atlantic or Air Crew Europe Stars, and then qualified for this award, received a bar "France and Germany." The only bar awarded with this Star is "Atlantic." This is again denoted by a silver rosette when wearing only ribbons.

In common with several of the other stars for the Second World War, this one could be gained without previously qualifying for the award of the 1939/45 Star. Service in the appropriate areas, between the end of the war with Germany and the Japanese surrender, could gain entitlement. This seems quite inappropriate if the main intention was to reward forces who had been engaged in some of the heaviest fighting of the whole war

Reverse

Defence Medal

The qualifying dates for this cupro-nickel medal were 3rd September 1939 to 2nd September 1945 and, contrary to popular belief, was harder to qualify for than some of the campaign stars. Generally speaking it was awarded for three years service in the United Kingdom or six months overseas in territories subjected to or threatened by enemy attack.

Like all other Second World War issues (except for those to Australians and S.Africans) it was unnamed.

When one considers that the Defence Medal symbolizes the courage of the civilian population during the 'Blitz' and the magnificent work of the Fire Services, Air Raid Precautions, Police, Ambulance Services and others, it is well worthy of inclusion in any collection. In fact, one could associate this medal with the George Cross awarded to Lieut. R. Davies, Royal Engineers, when he saved St. Paul's Cathedral by removing an unexploded bomb. This George Cross sold for £2,100.00 at Sotheby's in September, 1970.

War Medal

1939 — 1945

The qualifying period for this medal is the same as the Defence Medal, but it was only necessary to serve for twenty eight days in any of the Armed Forces to gain entitlement. In the case of the Merchant Navy the requirement was that the twenty eight days had to be served at sea.

Provision was made for operational service terminated by death, wounds, disability or capture. In such cases if the person had previously qualified for one of the campaign stars, the recipient was also entitled to the War Medal.

When mentioned in despatches, the bronze oak leaf emblem signifying this award, is worn on the ribbon of the War Medal, irrespective of the theatre of war in which it was gained. Only one oak leaf is worn, even if a recipient received more than on 'Mention.'

The Canadian issue was made in silver.

Reverse

Korea Medal

1950 — 1953

Although sanctioned by King George VI in 1951 this medal was issued later and the head of the present Queen is on the obverse.

There are two types, the second of which is much scarcer, as the legend changed from "Elizabeth II Dei. Gra: Britt: Omn: Regina F:D:" to "Elizabeth II: Dei: Gratia: Regina F:D: +". Medals to Canadian Forces have "Canada" below the head of the Queen, and are struck in silver, not cupro-nickel, as with the English issues.

Because of their gallant stand on the Imjim river, medals to the Gloucestershire regiment are most desirable, but there were several other outstanding actions.

The majority of medals are named in small impressed capitals, although the very few seen to the R.A.F. have been engraved, and the Australian and Canadian issues have their own type of naming, with possibly more than one style.

Reverse

Reverse

Campaign Service Medal

1962

This medal, which is never issued without bar, was authorised in October 1964, and replaces the Naval General Service Medal 1915–64 and General Service Medal (Army and R.A.F.) 1918–64. The undermentioned bars have so far been issued.

South Vietnam (December 1962–May 1964), Borneo (December 1962–August 1966), Radfan (April–July 1964), South Arabia (August 1964–November 1967), Malay Peninsula (August 1964–August 1966), Northern Ireland (August 1969–   ).

The South Vietnam bar, as far as is known, has only been awarded to Australian and New Zealand personnel, and is rare.

The fact that all three services now receive this medal is reflected in the type of naming, which now appears to be standard, irrespective of whether the recipient served in the R.N., Army or R.A.F. All medals examined have been named in small plain capitals.

Obverse

Vietnam Medal

1964—1973

The issue of this medal was authorised by their governments, in July 1968, for award to Australian and New Zealand personnel. The qualifying date was from 29th May, 1964, and entailed twenty eight days service in ships or one day on land with an operational unit. Official visits also counted, but had to total thirty days.

Many who received this medal also qualified for the star which was issued by the government of South Vietnam. To qualify, it was necessary to serve for six months in Vietnam.

Naming on the Vietnam medals that have been seen is in rather large and heavily impressed plain capitals. The South Vietnam medals have been rather crudely engraved. Only the regimental number, initial and surname are given. This applies to both medals.

Appendix

THE ORDER OF WEARING
ORDERS, DECORATIONS AND MEDALS

Lists of the approved order of wearing Orders, Decorations and Medals are published in the London Gazette from time to time. The first of these lists was published just after the 1914–18 War. The list below summarises the most up-to-date information. It includes Orders, Decorations and Medals which are no longer awarded; these Orders, Decorations and Medals have been so marked.

When the ribbon or miniature of a higher class of a junior Order is worn with the junior class of a senior Order, it is the class of the order which designates the precedence of the wearing.

For the purpose of record Orders, Decorations and Medals not mentioned in this book have nevertheless been included in the list.

𝔙𝔦𝔠𝔱𝔬𝔯𝔦𝔞 𝔠𝔯𝔬𝔰𝔰
𝔊𝔢𝔬𝔯𝔤𝔢 𝔠𝔯𝔬𝔰𝔰

Order of the Garter
Order of the Thistle
†Order of St. Patrick
Order of the Bath (1st, 2nd and 3rd class)
Order of Merit (Ranks next after 1st class of the Bath)
†Order of the Star of India (1st, 2nd and 3rd class)
Order of St. Michael and St. George (1st, 2nd and 3rd class)
†Order of the Indian Empire (1st, 2nd and 3rd class)
†Order of the Crown of India
Royal Victorian Order (1st, 2nd and 3rd class)
Order of the British Empire (1st, 2nd and 3rd class)
Order of the Companions of Honour (Ranks next after 1st class of the British Empire)
Distinguished Service Order
Royal Victorian Order (4th class)
Order of the British Empire (4th class)
Imperial Service Order
Royal Victorian Order (5th class)
Order of the British Empire (5th class)
†Indian Order of Merit (Military)
†Order of Burma (for gallantry)
Royal Red Cross (1st class)
Distinguished Service Cross
Military Cross
Distinguished Flying Cross
Air Force Cross
Royal Red Cross (2nd class)
†Order of British India
†Kaisar-i-Hind Medal
†Order of Burma (for meritorious service)
Order of St. John
*Albert Medal

†Union of South Africa King's Medal for Bravery (in gold)
Distinguished Conduct Medal
Conspicuous Gallantry Medal
George Medal
‡Queen's Police Medal (for gallantry)
‡Queen's Fire Service Medal (for gallantry)
*Edward Medal
†Royal West African Frontier Force Distinguished Conduct Medal
†King's African Rifles Distinguished Conduct Medal
†Indian Distinguished Service Medal
†Burma Gallantry Medal
†Union of South Africa King's Medal for Bravery (in silver)
Distinguished Service Medal
Military Medal
Distinguished Flying Medal
Air Force Medal
†Constabulary Medal (Ireland)
Board of Trade Medal (for saving life at sea)
†Indian Order of Merit (Civil)
*Empire Gallantry Medal
†Indian Police Medal for Gallantry
†Burma Police Medal for Gallantry
†Ceylon Police Medal for Gallantry
†Sierra Leone Police Medal for Gallantry
†Sierra Leone Fire Brigades Medal for Gallantry
†Colonial Police Medal for Gallantry
Queen's Gallantry Medal

*These medals are obsolete and living recipients were able to exchange their medals for the George Cross.
†These Orders, Decorations or Medals are no longer awarded but there may be living recipients.
‡These medals are only awarded posthumously.

(Continued)

†Uganda Services Medal (if awarded for
gallantry)
British Empire Medal
Canada Medal
Life Saving Medal of the Order of St. John
Queen's Police Medal for Distinguished Service
Queen's Fire Service Medal for Distinguished
Service
Queen's Medal for Chiefs
War Medals (in order of date of campaign)
Polar Medals (in order of date)
Royal Victorian Medal (in gold, silver or bronze)
Imperial Service Medal
Police Medals for Meritorious Service
†Uganda Services Medal (if awarded for
meritorious service)
Badge of Honour
Jubilee, Coronation and Durbar Medals
King George V Long and Faithful Service Medal
King George VI Long and Faithful Service
Medal
Queen Elizabeth II Long and Faithful Service
Medal
Efficiency and Long Service Decorations and
Medals, Medals for Champion Shots,
Independence, etc., Medals
Other Commonwealth Orders, Decorations and
Medals (instituted since 1949, otherwise than by
the Sovereign) and awards by the States of
Malaysia and the State of Brunei
Foreign Orders (in order of date of award)
Foreign Decorations (in order of date of award)
Foreign Medals (in order of date of award)

*These medals are obsolete and living recipients were able to
exchange their medals for the George Cross.
†These Orders, Decorations or Medals are no longer awarded
but there may be living recipients.
‡These medals are only awarded posthumously.

MENTIONS IN DESPATCHES

The system of mentioning specific acts of gallantry
or distinguished service under fire by senior officers
of their juniors in dispatches has been practised for
many years. We are here concerned with the emblems which denote that the wearer has been so
mentioned, which are a quite recent innovation.
Whereas the French award the Croix de Guerre
with an appropriate emblem to show the type of
dispatch in which the recipient has been mentioned
(Army, Corps, Division etc.,) the British had no
emblem until after the 1914–18 War when in 1920
King George V authorized the wearing of a multi
leaved oak emblem in bronze on the ribbon of the
Victory Medal of that War. In 1943 King George
VI authorized the wearing of a single leaved oak
emblem for those mentioned in dispatches during
the Second World War. Originally worn on the
jacket where medals would be worn, it was, after the
issue of the War Medal, authorized to be worn on
the ribbon of that medal. Emblems for Mentions in
other campaigns are worn on the appropriate
campaign ribbon or, if no medal is granted, on the
jacket after any other ribbons.

Index

Bibliography

Abbott (P. E.) and Tamplin (J. M. A.). British Gallantry Awards. London, 1971.

Carter (Thos.). Medals of the British Army and how they were won. London, 1861.

De La Bere (Brig. Sir Ivan). The Queen's Orders of Chivalry. London, 1961.

Dorling (Capt. H. Taprell). Ribbons and Medals. London 1916 onwards. Enlarged and revised editions, in association with L. F. Guille, 1956. 1963 edn.

Gordon (Major L. L.). British Battles and Medals. Aldershot, 1947. The 4th edition, London, 1971, has been revised by E. C. Joslin.

Gould (Robert). Campaign Medals of the British Army 1815–1972. London, 1972.

Hieronymussen (Paul). Orders, Medals and Decorations of Britain and Europe. London, 1967.

Irwin (D. Hastings). War Medals and Decorations, London, 1890.

Long (W. H.). Medals of the British Navy. London, 1895.

Mayo (J..H.). Medals and Decorations of the British Army and Navy. London, 1897.

Purves (A. A.). Collecting Medals and Decorations. Revised edition, 1971.

Risk (James C.). British Orders and Decorations, 1945 (The American Numismatic Society.).

Smyth (Sir John). The Story of the Victoria Cross, 1856–1963, London, 1963.

Smyth (Sir John). The Story of the George Cross. London, 1968.

Sreward (W. Augustus). War Medals and Their History. London, 1915.

Tancred (George). Historical Record of Medals Conferred on the British Navy, Army, and Auxiliary Forces. London, 1891.